lonely planet
kids

HIDDEN

WONDERS

A GUIDE TO
THE PLANET'S
WILDEST, WEIRDEST
PLACES

NICOLE MAGGI

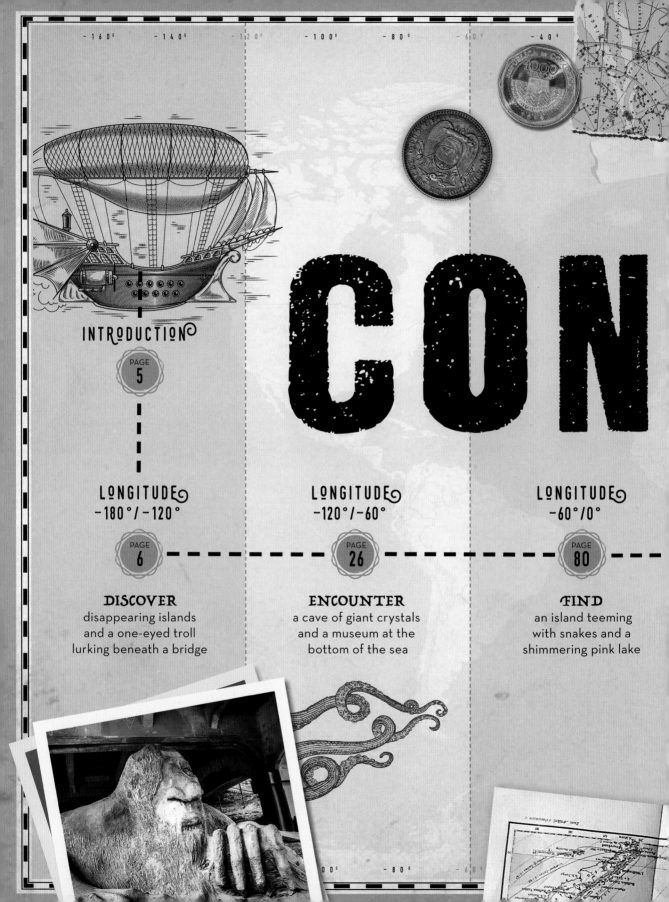

INTRODUCTION

CON

TENTS

INTRODUCTION

OH WONDROUS DISCOVERY!

You hold in your hands the shining key to some of the world's most secret places. Grab your compass and travel to the far reaches of this glorious planet. Descend into caves lit by glowworms brighter than the brightest chandelier. Uncover ancient history beneath the world's most romantic city. Float on waters as pink as a rose, swim with wild pigs on a pristine beach, and fly over the mouth of a volcano on the world's most daring swing.

Will you discover mermaids on a tiny island in South Korea, or witches deep in a Lithuanian forest? This book will take you everywhere and beyond. Each section includes all of the fascinating destinations you'll find at a specific line of longitude, those imaginary lines that divide the globe vertically and meet up at the North and South Poles.

So get ready to bungee jump off a road to nowhere in the Brazilian jungle, or lose yourself in the world's largest maze. Whether deep underwater in a prehistoric grotto or high on a cliff at the tip of a rock troll's tongue, adventure awaits around every corner. You have only to turn the page to discover it!

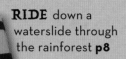

RIDE down a waterslide through the rainforest **p8**

DISCOVER THE TROLL
under the bridge **p23**

LONGITUDE
−180° / −120°

HIKE TO
the derailed train turned into an art installation
p20

ROLL UP YOUR SLEEVES~
we're going to clean up the shore along Plastic Beach **p17**

KICK YOUR SHOES OFF
...and throw 'em in a
tree **p25**

TREK TO THE SPOT
of a famous felled tree **p18**

VISIT THE
HAUNTED HOME
of a tortured gun-
fortune heiress **p24**

GO OFF THE RADAR
along California's Lost Coast **p15**

Taveuni, Fiji

WAITAVALA WATER SLIDE

Surf down on your feet or slide down on your butt. Whichever you choose, you'll whizz through the beautiful rainforest with surprising speed when you take a ride on the Waitavala Water Slide. Formed completely by natural forces, this fierce, slippery slope takes you down a chute along smooth rock formations in the jungles of Fiji. Your favorite water park's got nothing on this thrill ride.

TONGA
HUNGA TONGA-HUNGA HA'APAI

This tiny slice of land has the honor of being the world's youngest island. It lived as a quiet, underground volcano until 2015, when it burst out of the Pacific Ocean. The ash plumes from its eruption were so vast they diverted flights for days. When it settled down, it formed a seahorse-shaped island with a milky-green lake in the center of its crater. Alas, this baby island may only have a short life. Scientists believe that it's too fragile to survive more than a few decades. It won't be long before it erodes back into the ocean to resume its quiet, underwater life.

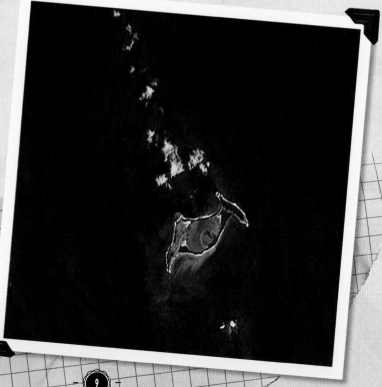

ALASKA, USA

ANIAKCHAK
NATIONAL
MONUMENT & PRESERVE

More people explore space each year than visit the otherworldly Aniakchak National Monument and Preserve. A collapsed volcanic crater, this barren landscape feels more than a little like a "lost world." Giant bears wander across the tundra. Clouds fill up the crater and spill over the edges like waterfalls. Only the most intrepid explorers hike down into the crater using animal trails, before whitewater rafting down the Aniakchak River out to Aniakchak Bay and the Pacific Ocean.

OAHU, HAWAII, USA

PINEAPPLE GARDEN MAZE

IT'S NOT HARD TO GET LOST in this labyrinth, which is over 39,000 sq ft (3,600 sq meter) long and was twice named the World's Largest Maze by the Guinness World Records. It's built entirely out of plants native to Hawaii. Race through hibiscus, panax, and pineapple plants to see if you can beat the fastest time recorded (seven minutes). Most people take about 45 minutes to complete the maze, but why rush when you're surrounded by all this beauty?

Oahu, Hawaii, USA

HA'IKU STAIRS

IT'S A STAIRWAY TO

nowhere, but at the top of these 3,922 steps you'll think you've reached heaven. The stairway once led to a top-secret radio facility in the 1940s, but after the radio base was shut down, the stairs remained. Although you're not supposed to climb these stairs, that doesn't stop risk-takers from hiking up for a spectacular view from the top of the Ko'olau Mountain Range. Paradise, indeed!

13

KIRITIMATI

When Captain Cook landed here on Christmas Day in 1777, he named the island after the holiday. Kiritimati, pronounced "Krismas" in the Kiribati language because the "ti" sounds like an "s," in English, is the world's biggest coral atoll. As remote as it is, it's populated with more birds than people.

On Christmas Island, you can visit London, Paris, and Poland without even buying a plane ticket. Those are the names of three of the island's four early settlements. The island was a former British colony, so the name London makes sense. As for Paris and Poland? The French owner of a coconut plantation named them for his home country, and the home of his Polish engineer. The fourth settlement? It's called Banana! It's the site of the first banana groves, so the name makes sense, though you may giggle every time you say it.

CALIFORNIA, USA

CALIFORNIA'S LOST COAST

THERE ARE STILL PLACES here that remain untouched. Up in northern California, Route 1 turns inland to avoid coastline that's too rugged for a highway. If you're not scared off by the unpaved logging roads, keep along the water—and you'll discover the Lost Coast.

From spectacular cliffs to windswept beaches, the Lost Coast is a 62-mile (100km) stretch of California that is virtually off the radar because it's so hard to get to. But if you put in the work, you might find yourself camping in an abandoned settler's cabin and gazing up at old-growth redwood trees. Don't be alarmed if a herd of elk graze past you as you hike across lonely but mesmerizing landscapes, from the Sinkyone Wilderness State Park to the King Range National Conservation Area. This is a place worth preserving, to keep it a hidden wonder for generations to come.

MAUI, HAWAII, USA

PU'UPIHA CEMETERY

IT LOOKS LIKE EVERY OTHER relaxing Hawaiian beach—except for the gravestones. Outside of the town of Lahaina on Maui's west coast, the "Cemetery in the Sand" tells a story of Hawaiian history. In the late 1800s, large numbers of Chinese and Japanese immigrants flocked to Hawaii seeking work in the sugar industry. When they died, their bones were sent back home to Asia to be buried. But as the years passed, the Asian community began to bury their dead in Hawaii and chose this spot on the beach as their final resting place. One side of Pu'upiha Cemetery is Chinese and the other is Japanese. On the Chinese side, small stone posts mark the plots. The Japanese side is marked by large headstones. When you're here, you feel something spiritual about the spot. In fact, beyond the wharf is an ancient Hawaiian burial site, proof that this has been a sacred place for centuries.

Big Island, Hawaii, USA
PLASTIC BEACH

The official name of this beach is Kamilo Beach, which translates to "swirling currents" in Hawaiian. It's fitting, since the powerful combination of tides and trade winds here have delivered all sorts of things to the shore. In times past, logs arrived from the Pacific Northwest, which the Hawaiians used to make canoes. More recently the flotsam that's arrived here hasn't been so useful. Tons of plastic garbage from the "Great Pacific Garbage Patch" have washed up on the beach, which is now nicknamed Plastic Beach. It's a harsh reminder of how wasteful humans can be, and a lesson in the power of nature and how much work we still have to do to protect it.

BRITISH COLUMBIA, CANADA

THE FELLED GOLDEN
SPRUCE

Among a sea of green in the Haida Gwaii forest, a bright yellow spruce tree stood out like a single sunflower in a meadow. Its golden color was caused by a genetic mutation that deprived the tree of the chlorophyll (green pigment) usually found in spruce trees. The tree, pictured at right, was 164ft (50km) high, and played an important role in the legends of the indigenous Haida people. That is, until 1997, when an environmental activist cut it down . . . to protest cutting down trees! You can hike the Golden Spruce Trail to visit the trunk of the once mighty tree on the riverbank. Despite its fall, the tree lives on. Cuttings were taken from it and spread all across British Columbia. Someday the little sprucelings will be as tall and golden as their mom once was.

WHISTLER TRAIN WRECK SITE

Street art in the middle of the forest? That's what was created when some local graffiti artists started spraying their work across abandoned train carriages in a forest outside the city. It all started in 1956, when a train was traveling too fast through the canyon and derailed. A logging company cleared the railroad by dragging the wrecked train cars into the woods, where they were left to rust. Over the years, local artists came in and transformed the place into a colorful art installation.

A suspension bridge crosses the Cheakamus River, leading you to the artsy wreck site. But it's not just for artists! Mountain bikers have also made use of the site, building jumps and rails around the trains to create a woodsy bike playground.

San Francisco, California, USA

THE WAVE ORGAN

WITH THIS INTERACTIVE piece of art, you don't just see the bay, you hear the bay. Standing on a small jetty, you can take in views of the Golden Gate Bridge and the infamous Alcatraz Island prison. Keep your ears open and you can hear the 25 organ pipes that artist Peter Richards installed at various levels around the jetty. As the water rushes in and out of the pipes, notes come out! Stand on this masterpiece with the wind in your hair and listen to the sea sing you its song.

TUALATIN, OREGON, USA

THE GIANT PUMPKIN REGATTA

Every October, people gather for the West Coast Giant Pumpkin Regatta—where competitors carve out the center of a giant pumpkin (and we do mean giant), get inside, and race across the lake. Pumpkins aren't particularly seaworthy, which is half the fun! The sight of them bobbing and bouncing in the water is what makes this race so special. The fastest pumpkin (and the paddler who manages to stay inside it) wins!

SEATTLE, WASHINGTON, USA

FREMONT PUBLIC SCULPTURES

Step into the weird and wonderful Seattle neighborhood of Fremont. The community motto here is *de libertas quirkas*—freedom to be peculiar—and the residents here take that to heart. The tree-lined streets are regular victims of "art attacks": sculptures and exhibits that pop up overnight and disappear as quickly as they come. There are several permanent pieces around the 'hood as well. These include a giant stone troll hidden beneath a bridge and a Cold War rocket that never took off. It's a Fremont tradition to dress these statues up, so chances are when you see them they'll be wearing something festive!

SAN JOSE, CALIFORNIA, USA
WINCHESTER MYSTERY HOUSE

When her husband died, Sarah inherited the Winchester family fortune—made off of the invention of the Winchester rifle. That money came at a price, though. The legend goes that Sarah believed she was being haunted by the spirits of people who had been shot and killed by Winchester rifles. When a psychic told her that she needed to outwit the spirits in order to survive, Sarah got to work.

She bought an unfinished farmhouse in San Jose, California, and had workmen renovating the house 24 hours a day for 38 years. Staircases lead to nowhere, doors open onto brick walls, and sometimes the only way into a room is through a cabinet. Always trying to stay one step ahead of the ghosts, Sarah slept in a different room every night—there are 160 of them in the house! It is said that she often wore a veil and held nightly séances.

Sarah died peacefully in her sleep, at age 82. Her house was auctioned off to the highest bidder, who turned it into a tourist attraction.

HIGHWAY 50, NEVADA, USA
THE SHOE TREE

CALLED THE LONELIEST Road, Highway 50 stretches for miles through empty desert—until you get to the Shoe Tree! Legend has it that a newlywed couple got into a fight beneath the tree. The bride threatened to walk home and the groom tossed her shoes into the tree to prevent her from leaving! They made up, and a tradition was born. People threw their shoes up into the tree for years, until the original tree was cut down in 2010. Now a nearby cottonwood named Shoe Tree Junior does the job. If you find yourself traveling down the Loneliest Road, make sure to bring an old pair of shoes to add to the story.

MEET THE
CRYSTAL
MAIDEN~
she's calcified
but cool
p37

SWING ACROSS
the edge of the world **p51**

LONGITUDE
−120°/−60°

PADDLE ALONGSIDE
these little piggies **p55**

SNORKEL THROUGH
an underwater
museum **p42**

VIEW
ANCIENT
CARVINGS
from high in
the sky **p59**

JOURNEY TO HELL
and back . . . literally **p47**

MEET A WITCH
with a guinea pig at
this market **p53**

**DESCEND
UNDERGROUND**
to a cavern of
enormous
crystals
p32

CREEP ALONG
a post-apocalyptic
graveyard **p40**

DEATH VALLEY NATIONAL PARK, CALIFORNIA, USA
RACETRACK PLAYA

You don't get the name "Death Valley" without some serious street cred. Situated in the northern part of Death Valley National Park is an unpaved danger zone called Racetrack Road that cuts through 27mi (43km) of vast desert. It leads to the Racetrack Playa, a huge dry lake bed dotted with boulders. But these aren't just any ordinary boulders. These rocks, some as heavy as 700lb (318kg), can move, leaving tracks in the dirt!

How, you ask? The movement of the rocks was a mystery until 2014 when scientists finally solved it.

It has to do with the extreme temperatures of the area. In the winter, a thin layer of ice covers the playa. On sunny days, the ice cracks and winds rush down from the mountains, pushing the ice sheets apart. When the ice completely melts, the boulders are left in their new positions. Even though we now know the secret of this place, that doesn't take away from its stark beauty.

NILAND, CALIFORNIA, USA

SALVATION MOUNTAIN

THE SALTON SEA IS A desolate wilderness in the baking California desert. But just east of that desolation is this colorful living prayer built right onto a low mesa (flat-topped hill). It was the life's work of a man named Leonard Knight. Born in Vermont in 1931, he drifted around the United States until 1967, when he had a religious epiphany and decided he wanted to share his passion with the world. Using his bare hands, he built an adobe (mud brick) and straw mountain onto the mesa, and topped it with a gleaming white cross. The hill is painted with every color of the rainbow and bears messages like "God is Love." It's estimated that over 100,000 gallons (379,000L) of paint were used to coat Salvation Mountain. You can wind through a surreal maze painted with neon trees, visit a garden of trees, flowers, and waterfalls, and stop by a graveyard of abandoned vehicles, all covered with countless prayers. Leonard Knight died in 2014, but a group of volunteers maintains the mountain and take donations of paint to help keep the place colorful and gleaming.

@UTAH, USA

NINE MILE CANYON

TUCKED AWAY IN THE RED

sandstone mountains of the Utah wilderness sits one of the world's largest and most ancient art galleries. Running along the walls of this canyon—which actually stretches for 46mi (74km)—are thousands of ancient hieroglyphs that were carved and painted into the rocks by the native Fremont and Ute tribes who lived here between 600 and 1800 AD. The scenes tell a story of what life was like for Native tribes, showing everything from war to farmwork and family life. You can also visit the homes they lived in, called pit houses, which are remarkably still intact after all these centuries.

MARIETA ISLANDS, MEXICO

HIDDEN BEACH

True to its name, Hidden Beach can't be seen from the outside and is only accessible through a long water tunnel that links it to the Pacific Ocean. If you were to swim or kayak through the tunnel, you'd arrive at a doughnut-hole-shaped beach, surrounded by cream-colored sand. The island's strange shape is rumored to be the result of modern bomb testing by the Mexican government, though scientists have many theories.

CHIHUAHUA, MEXICO

CAVE OF THE CRYSTALS

Almost 20 years ago, two brothers working at a mining company stumbled onto what seemed like the set of a science-fiction movie. Enormous, translucent crystals crisscrossed the interior of a cave nearly 1,000ft (304m) below the ground. The cave was once flooded with water, but when the mining company pumped it dry, the 500,000-year-old crystals were uncovered. They're the largest crystals found on the planet and made of the mineral selenite, which is so soft you can scratch it with your fingernail. After its discovery, researchers visited the cave wearing special suits to protect them from the blazing temperatures, which could reach up to 120°F (49°C). It was impossible to stay in the cave unprotected for more than a few minutes.

In 2017 mining operations ceased and water was released back into the cave, allowing the crystals to start growing again. But flooding it with water means no human can enter, and the crystals are currently lost to us once more.

EASTER ISLAND, CHILE

THE NAVEL OF THE WORLD

FOR SUCH A TINY SPECK of land, Easter Island is crammed with an amazing number of archaeological sites. The most famous of these are the moai, giant human statues, that are scattered all over the island like eerie guardians from another world. Yet one of the most fascinating things on Easter Island is a perfectly round stone surrounded by four smaller round stones. Legend has it that King Hotu Matu'a, the first settler of Easter Island, brought the stone here to represent the "navel of the world." Meaning, if the earth was shaped like a body, this would be its belly button! That's not the only curious thing about the stone: it's also magnetic. If you place your compass on the rock, it will lose its direction. Just another eternal mystery from this extraordinary island.

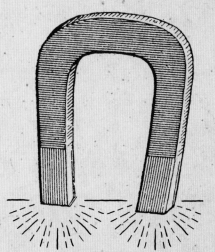

NEAR SANTA FE, NEW MEXICO, USA

RA PAULETTE'S SANDSTONE CAVES

THERE'S A HIDDEN WORLD underneath the New Mexico desert, and it's all man-made. Artist Ra Paulette has spent over 25 years carving out a series of underground caves in the soft sandstone rock. It's slow and lonely work; he uses only hand tools (no power drills for him!) and has only his pet dog for company. Within these caves, he's dug chambers and tunnels, crafted doorways and staircases, and sculpted figures and plants. Amazingly, he's even chiseled an entire cavern with a tree-like figure in the center—making for a completely fantastical landscape. There are over a dozen caves so far, all lit by huge natural skylights.

NEBRASKA, USA

CARHENGE

Inspired by famous ancient Stonehenge in England, Carhenge is made out of—you guessed it—cars. American artist Jim Reinders decided to memorialize his father with this towering tribute. Dedicated in 1987, the ginormous sculpture is made out of 39 classic American automobiles. These cars were painted gray and assembled in the exact same formation as Stonehenge, except we definitely know who built Carhenge—and how!

CAYO, BELIZE

ACTUN TUNICHIL MUKNAL

Journey almost a mile (1.6km) underground into this vast cavern full of history. A thousand years ago, the ancient Maya tried to find a route to the underworld through this cave. Inside are huge stalagmites and stalactites, along with broken pots that were once used to offer food—or blood—to the gods. But even more unique and disturbing? Over a dozen skeletons were found here, and believed to be a part of ancient human sacrifices. Most eerie of all is the Crystal Maiden, the skeleton of a young woman that's completely calcified. Her sparkling bones embody just why the Maya might have chosen this mystical place as their channel to the gods.

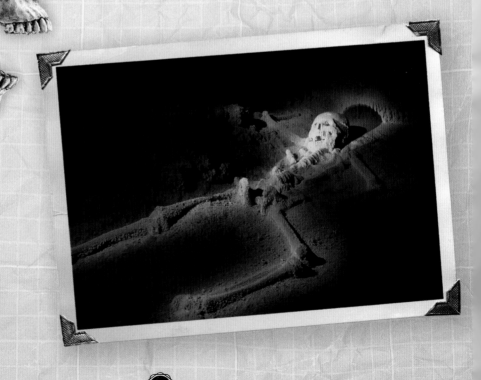

PETERSBURG, KENTUCKY, USA

ABANDONED GHOST SHIP

Y ou would never know by look-ing at this abandoned ship that it has such a colorful past! In 1902 the boat was ordered to be built by a wealthy railroad tycoon to serve as his luxury yacht. Later it was sold to the US Navy, which used it to sink U-boats during WWI. The Navy then loaned it to none other than Thomas Edison, who conducted military research aboard the ship off the east coast of the US.

After the war, the ship was used as a fishing boat before returning to military service during WWII. Once its fighting days were over, it spent over 40 years as a tour boat in New York City. After that, it was sold one last time to a Cincinnati resident, who sailed it down the Ohio River and left it to rot where the Ohio meets Taylor Creek. Now in its final resting place, it's a quiet end for a ship with so much history. But when you come upon it floating in the river, you can just imagine its former glory.

WHITE, GEORGIA, USA

OLD CAR CITY

People sure love their cars . . . even the junkers. Over 4,000 of these beloved rust-mobiles languish here in Old Car City, and the forest has reclaimed many of them. It's one part junkyard, one part classic car museum, and one part nature preserve, with 6mi (9.65km) of nature trails winding through the area. Take a glimpse into what might happen to our cars in a post-apocalyptic world.

Zarcero, Costa Rica

PARQUE FRANCISCO ALVARADO

TAKE A STROLL IN THIS lovely park in Costa Rica and you'll notice something unusual about the topiaries. Stretching out from a 17th-century church, the park is filled with surreal shapes and figures. In the 1960s the gardener Evangelisto Blanco decided to let his imagination run wild. He shaped the hedges into melting archways, friendly dinosaurs, and otherworldly creatures. The garden continues to thrive today thanks to Blanco's creativity.

ROATÁN, HONDURAS

BAY ISLANDS UNDERWATER MUSEUM

IF YOU THINK MUSEUMS are oh-so-boring, then you've never been to this one. What's so unusual about it, you ask? The exhibits are all underwater! Kick off your sneakers, pull on a pair of flippers, and dive into the sparkling waters off the coast of Roatán in Honduras. Beneath the surface you'll find Maya statues and artifacts, a Spanish galleon, and more in this underwater scavenger hunt.

ATLANTA, GEORGIA, USA

CENTERS FOR DISEASE CONTROL MUSEUM

IF YOU'VE EVER WATCHED a zombie movie, chances are you've heard of the CDC. Whether it's a flu epidemic or an Ebola outbreak, the CDC is in charge of national health security in the United States. This museum in Atlanta showcases the CDC's achievements in disease prevention, treatment, and research. It's very reassuring to know that when the apocalypse comes, the CDC will be ready.

Diquís Delta, Costa Rica

DIQUÍS SPHERES

These giant stone spheres are all that's left of the mysterious Diquís civilization that existed in Costa Rica from 700 BC to 1530 AD. What they were used for, no one knows. But the way that some of the stones are aligned suggests that they may have been solar calendars. Or they may have been used to show off power: the bigger the rock, the stronger the chief! Either way, they continue to mystify those wandering among the spheres in public parks and museums on the west coast of Costa Rica.

MORGANTOWN, GEORGIA, USA

TANK TOWN USA

TANK TOWN USA'S MOTTO IS "Drive Tanks. Crush Cars." That pretty much sums it up. Here, visitors can drive tanks . . . over cars! You can also take a spin on a 20-ton (18-metric-ton) construction excavator and dig some holes. If you're obsessed with tanks, this place is a dream!

GRAND CAYMAN, CAYMAN ISLANDS

HELL

JOURNEY TO HELL AND back—literally. Tucked away on the heavenly island of Grand Cayman is a place called Hell, which contains a group of ancient limestone formations. These spiky black rocks definitely look like they've risen up out of the underworld. Although the barren landscape is at odds with the rest of this tropical paradise, the locals embrace it. The post office and gift shop welcome you with a bright red "Welcome to Hell" sign, and you can meet "Satan" here. (Okay, it's actually a guy named Ivan Farrington, but it's still pretty hellish around here!)

HAVANA, CUBA
FUSTERLANDIA

In the 1990s, Cuban artist José Fuster decided to spruce up his house. But his DIY project soon spilled beyond his own home, eventually covering several city blocks and was nicknamed Fusterlandia. See the bright ceramics complete with imaginative paintings, detailed tile work, and sensuous sculptures in every color of the rainbow.

There's a Cuban theme to the sprawling artwork. Inside a huge mural painting of the *Granma* yacht, you can spot important historical figures Fidel Castro, Che Guevara, and Camilo Cienfuegos. Reproductions of the Cuban flag are everywhere. A line of houses have the words "Viva Cuba" emblazoned on their chimneys.

The brightest spot in the whole 'hood is Fuster's own house. Murals cover every surface. There are sculpted arches and swirling ceramic trees too! In the center of it all, there is a pool painted like an undersea fantasy with mermaids, fishermen, and a giant octopus.

NEAR MIAMI, FLORIDA, USA

CORAL CASTLE

THIS MASSIVE SCULPTURE

garden in Florida is as mysterious as it is astounding. It was a labor of love for Latvian immigrant Edward Leedskalnin, who created these sculptures after being rejected by his promised bride. He made them entirely by hand out of coral stone local to Florida. But *how* he did it remains a mystery—he worked at night by lantern light so no one could watch him. While Leedskalnin came from a family of stonemasons in Latvia, modern scholars still don't know how he built this immense park on his own since many of the sculptures are carved out of a single piece of stone, and some of them reach over 25ft (8m) tall. Just how *did* one man wield such massive rocks?

TUNGURAHUA PROVINCE, ECUADOR

THE SWING AT THE END OF THE WORLD

Way up high in the Ecuadorian jungle is the world's most perilous treehouse. Perched on the edge of a canyon, the Casa de Arbol is actually a seismic observation station. It's there to keep an eye on its next-door neighbor Tungurahua, an active volcano. But the best part of the treehouse is its swing. Hanging from a tree branch, it's just a little plank of wood suspended by two ropes. And unlike the swings at your local playground, there's no harness, net, or any safety features at all. People who do brave the swing, though, are rewarded with an incredible view of the canyon.

Nariño, Colombia

SANTUARIO DE LAS LAJAS

Hanging over a canyon, the Las Lajas Sanctuary in Colombia looks like a miracle, and legend has it that's how it was founded. According to the locals, in 1754 an Amerindian woman and her deaf-mute daughter were caught in a storm here. They took shelter in the gorge and in the midst of the wind and rain, they saw the image of the Virgin Mary in the rocks. The daughter suddenly became able to hear and speak. And so a humble chapel was built on this spot. Pilgrims traveled from far and wide to the shrine in search of healing. Finally in 1949 the grand cathedral was built. It perches over the Guáitara River, connected to the ravine by a bridge. It may not be humble anymore, but its appearance is still miraculous.

LIMA, PERU

LIMA WITCHES' MARKET

THE WOMEN COME FROM the mountains and they arrive at dawn. They wear traditional layered petticoats and bowler hats—an outfit identifying them as *curanderos*, mystical healers . . . or witches.

The witches come to the market in Lima once a week to practice their craft: healing. This traditional folk medicine is a blend of Catholicism, Santeria, and folk superstition, and it's been unchanged for centuries. Lima is a modern city, but there is still a deep belief in the old ways here. Even so, the *curanderos* roll with the times, and above their booths are banners that list their websites.

Each healer specializes in something different, from mending broken bones to curing cancer. They use a variety of tools, but the most notable (and cutest) is a guinea pig. These adorable rodents identify the patient's ailment and from there a treatment is carried out, ranging from laying hands on a broken bone to passing an egg over a cancerous tumor, all while chanting and praying. A line of people wait to be healed, applauding as each person leaves.

LIMA, PERU

MUSEO DEL CEREBRO

This museum in Lima is a zombie's heaven. In a plain building behind the Institute of Neurological Science is a collection of more than 3,000 brains. They're all contained in neatly labeled and formaldehyde-filled jars. Each brain displays the damage caused by various diseases. Diana Rivas is a neuropathologist, someone who studies diseases of the nervous system, and heads the museum. She also performs autopsies here, collecting new specimens to put on display. While most visitors are medical students, anyone who wants to learn more about the most interesting organ in our bodies can visit.

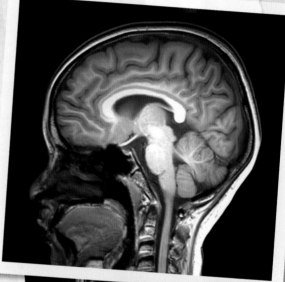

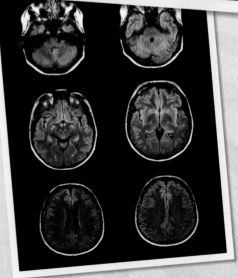

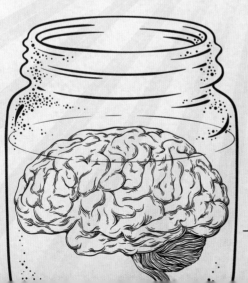

Big Major Cay, The Bahamas

PIG BEACH

You've heard the expression "happy as a pig in mud" but what about "happy as a pig in seawater"? On this uninhabited part of Big Major Cay in the Bahamas, that's just what you'll find—a bunch of cute piggy paddlers. No one knows how the pigs got here in the first place. Were they survivors of a shipwreck carrying livestock to Nassau? Did some seafaring explorer bring the pigs here? However they arrived, these pigs are wild but friendly, and love the ocean more than any muddy farm.

ANTIOQUIA, COLOMBIA

LA CUEVA DEL ESPLENDOR

What's the best thing to do after a long hike? If you answered "jump in a pool," you'll love this Cave of Splendor near the small town of Jardín in Colombia. There's a hiking or horseback-riding route through lush green mountains which comes to a steep riverbed trail. The reward for all that exercise? This glorious cave. Worn down by the rushing water over hundreds of years, a waterfall tumbles through the roof. The deep, refreshing water at the base of the waterfall is the perfect place to take a plunge and cool off.

San Antonio del Tequendama, Colombia

TEQUENDAMA FALLS MUSEUM

THIS MUSEUM STARTED out as a 1920s luxury hotel that overlooked the magnificent Tequendama Falls. But plans to expand into a resort failed, and the empty hotel fell into disrepair as the falls became polluted with trash and sewage from the nearby capital of Bogotá.

In recent years the Institute of Natural Sciences of the University of Colombia and the Ecological Farm Foundation of Porvenir took it on as a joint project, and in 2013 the hotel was reborn as a museum of biodiversity and culture. Now the Bogotá River and Tequendama Falls are being cleaned up too. With hard work and a little luck, the museum will see a cleaner and brighter next 100 years.

ANTIOQUIA, COLOMBIA

EL PEÑÓL DE GUATAPÉ

THIS GIANT STONE RISES 650ft (200m) into the air over the green hills surrounding it in Colombia. It's so out of place that the indigenous Tahamies people worshipped it centuries ago. But it wasn't until 1954 that someone actually made it to the top of the rock. A group of friends wedged boards into the single crack running down the length of the stone. It took them five days, but they finally made it all the way to the summit. Now visitors can take the same trip up, using a stone staircase that's been built into the same crack, with stunning views of the surrounding lakes and islands from the lookout tower at the top.

Nazca Desert, Peru

NAZCA LINES

Take a flight above the Nazca Desert in Peru and you'll see more than sand and rock. High above the ground, animals carved into the earth will take shape beneath you: a monkey with a curved tail, a hummingbird with a long thin beak, and a spider the size of a skyscraper. All are etched into the landscape here, scattered over a 310-sq-mile (803 sq km) stretch of plain.

It's believed these carvings were created by ancient Nazca people who lived here from 200 BC to 500 AD. The lines and shapes scattered over this stretch of the Nazca Plain remain an archaeological mystery. They were made by removing earth and rocks from the desert, exposing the light-colored sand beneath. The designs have stayed intact for so long due to the dryness of the climate, without much rain, wind, or erosion.

But because the huge etchings can't be seen from the ground, it wasn't until the dawn of air travel in the 1930s that pilots began to spot them from the sky. How did the Nazca people create these perfect designs without being able to see them fully? And why were they created in the first place? One theory is that the geometric shapes may have been used to beg the gods for water in this very dry place.

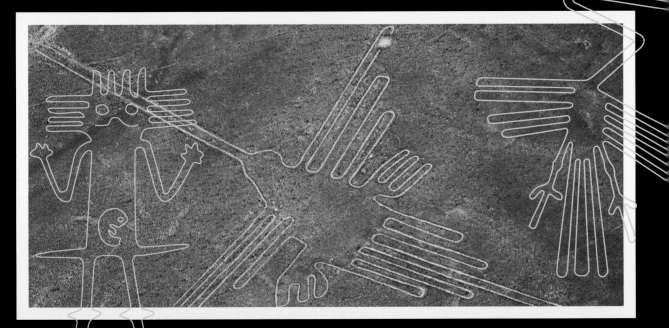

ASSATEAGUE ISLAND, VIRGINIA, USA

ASSATEAGUE ISLAND'S
FERAL
HORSES

These carefree "Chincoteague ponies" roam the coastline in groups, though no one is quite sure how they got here. The dreamy theory is that the horses are the descendants of survivors from a shipwreck off the Virginia coast. Another explanation is that, originally, the herds were kept on the island so their owners could get out of paying taxes on them. Despite their feral upbringing, the horses are actually quite gentle.

ZIPAQUIRÁ, COLOMBIA

CATEDRAL DE SAL

Cathedrals are made out of brick and stone, right? Not this one. The Colombian cathedral was carved by removing 250,000 tons (228,000 metric tons) of salt and is one of only three salt cathedrals in the world. Descend over 600ft (183m) belowground into a salt mine and you'll find yourself inside a stunning sanctuary. Intricate Catholic symbolism fill the series of 14 chapels that make up the church. Dramatic lighting adds to the moody atmosphere, especially in the central nave. There, a mammoth cross shines from top to bottom, casting a truly heavenly glow.

SLEEPY HOLLOW, NEW YORK, USA
SLEEPY HOLLOW CEMETERY

You might have heard the Legend of Sleepy Hollow and the Headless Horseman. But did you know that Sleepy Hollow is a real place? North of New York City lies an idyllic stretch of the Hudson Valley with some of the best apple picking in the country, and a rich history that dates back before the Revolutionary War.

In the Sleepy Hollow Cemetery, rows of weathered gravestones sink into the ground. Some plots contain famous names in American history: Rockefeller, Carnegie, and the author of "The Legend of Sleepy Hollow" himself, Washington Irving, are all buried here. The cemetery has even been used as a backdrop in creepy television shows (*Dark Shadows*) and moody music videos (the Ramones). There's no denying its gloomy, atmospheric appeal, but you wouldn't want to linger too long after midnight here or you may find yourself running from the Headless Horseman who made this place famous.

PATAGONIA, CHILE
CUEVA DEL MILODÓN NATURAL MONUMENT

Whichever method you choose, once you arrive you'll be greeted by the statue of a giant sloth at the entrance. The statue is a reminder of some of the remains and fossils found in the area—giant sloths (called *Mylodon*) and saber-toothed cats (called *Smilodon*) once also roamed here.

Catch a glimpse of what life was like in 6000 BC in these remote caves in Chile's Patagonia region. Getting here is half the adventure, whether you take a bumpy flight, a very long bus ride, or a boat through stunning fjords.

ꞰMARAS, ꝐERU

MORAY

THE INCANS WERE KNOWN for their masterful engineering, and this amphitheater is no exception. In a remote part of the Sacred Valley, grass-covered terraces are carved into the landscape—designed and positioned in relation to the sun and wind. There's actually a difference in temperature from the top of the bowl to the bottom, meaning the climate on each terrace varies slightly. In fact each terrace corresponds to different growing conditions across what was the Incan Empire. It's likely they used the terraces to test different crops, studying which climate was best suited to grow potato, maize, or quinoa. Talk about amazing technology!

CHILOÉ, CHILE

DOCK OF SOULS

THE DOCK OF SOULS

looks like a dock to nowhere. Located on the island of Chiloé in southern Chile, the wooden pier curves toward the edge of a cliff and ends abruptly with a drop to the sea. It looks like a mistake, but it's actually a sculpture by Chilean artist Marcelo Orellana Rivera. He was inspired by the indigenous Mapuche people's legend of Tempilcahue. According to the myth, Tempilcahue ferried the souls of the dead across the water to the afterlife. Sit on the edge of the Dock of Souls at sunset and you can just imagine Tempilcahue pulling up to the dock in his ferry, ready to take waiting souls to the beyond.

CAICOS CONCH FARM

YOU WON'T FIND A petting zoo here. Instead you'll find the world's only farm dedicated to raising sea snails. Conch is an important staple in the Caribbean menu. You can find it in any restaurant here served in a number of delicious ways: fried, chopped into fresh ceviche salad, or grilled. On this farm in the Turks and Caicos Islands, you can get a glimpse of just how these conches go from farm to table. The farm also features two mascots, Sally and Jerry—two full-grown conches you can say hello to.

CARHUÉ, ARGENTINA

VILLA EPECUÉN

ONE OF THE SALTIEST lakes in the world, Lake Epecuén drew tourists to its healing waters for decades. Luxury hotels, fancy restaurants, and swanky nightclubs lined its shores. People flocked to the Argentinian resort town between the 1920s and the 1970s. But in 1985 a natural catastrophe disrupted everything. Changing weather patterns caused a seiche, or standing wave, and the dam on the lake broke. The salty waters slowly swallowed the whole town and soon every building was underwater.

It wasn't until 2009 that the waters finally receded. In their place was a damp ghost town covered in a thin layer of sea salt. What's left is little more than a pile of concrete rubble and a forest of dead trees. The strange remains of Villa Epecuén have fascinated archaeologists and photographers. Only one lonely person lives there, Pablo Novak, keeping alive the glamour that was drowned so long ago.

CANAS, PERU

Q'ESWACHAKA ROPE BRIDGE

When the Incas lived here 600 years ago, they used rope bridges to cross canyons and rivers. Now the Q'eswachaka Bridge is the last one left. It's made out of *ichu* (a type of grass) and hangs high above the Apurímac River. But don't fear, the bridge is remade every June by the local Quechua communities. The bridge ropes are woven by the women of the communities, then collected at a yearly festival and braided together by the *chakarauwaq* (engineers). The old bridge is dropped into the river and replaced by the new one—then a ceremony takes place, to thank the mountain spirits for the continued safety of anyone who crosses this wondrous bridge.

Valparaiso, Chile

PUNTA PITE

TAKE A STROLL UNLIKE ANY other along this stunning patch of Chile's Central Coast. Nature and art blend seamlessly together where stone pathways are built into the granite cliffs. Wind along the 1-mile (1.6km) route from a pebble beach to swimming holes that lead out to the ocean, squeeze through narrow passages, then climb up stone staircases to the top of a cliff—where cypress trees and sculptures are on full display. Up here, it's hard to keep track of where nature ends and art begins.

Uyuni, Bolivia

CEMENTERIO DE TRENES

High up on the Andean plateau in Bolivia there lies a train graveyard. During the 19th century the town of Uyuni was a major transportation hub for mining companies. British railway lines were built to connect the town to ports in the Pacific Ocean, and trains ran back and forth from the mines to the ports. But by the mid-20th century, mining was no longer profitable and Britain wasn't particularly welcome in the area. The trains were no use anymore, so were abandoned and left here to rust.

CULEBRA, PUERTO RICO

TANKS OF FLAMENCO BEACH

On this beautiful stretch of beach, two decommissioned tanks sit still in the sand. Although Flamenco Beach is now a perfectly laid-back place to soak up some sun, back in the late 1930s the US Navy decided it was the perfect place to practice war. Bombing practice and military exercises took place here for decades, and got more intense during the Vietnam War. By 1971 the Culebra locals had had enough— their protests led to the US Navy ceasing all military activity on the beach.

The two tanks are all that remain of the military's presence. Puerto Ricans have covered them with graffiti art; today they remain a colorful symbol of the power of resistance.

SUCRE, BOLIVIA

PARQUE CRETÁCICO

Get ready to cast your mind way, way back. Once upon a time 68 million years ago, dinosaurs roamed the earth here in Sucre, Bolivia. Over 5,000 footprints travel the Cal Orck'o cliff wall—*Hadrosaurs*, *Ceratops*, and *Tyrannosaurus rex* all once walked here. Their footprints are preserved in hardened stone that was once soft clay. There are even prints of a baby *T. rex*, along with skeletons of several dinosaurs in the rock. The perfect place to marvel at relics from the land before time, here sits the largest collection of dinosaur prints in the whole world.

VIRGIN ISLANDS, USA

TEKTITE UNDERWATER HABITAT

IT'S A PLOT STRAIGHT OUT of a science-fiction movie: a group of "aquanauts" living in a bunker underwater, studying the effects of living in an extreme environment, and reporting the results to the government. But in 1969, this actually happened. The US government wanted to know what happens to humans when they're thrown together in a small space under extreme conditions. They installed two metal cylinders at the bottom of the ocean off the island of St John in the Caribbean. Then they gathered four scientists who lived in the cylinders for 60 days. The crew breathed 92% nitrogen and 8% oxygen for the length of their mission (in comparison, we breathe 78% nitrogen and 21% oxygen in our air every day). At the end of the mission they spent 19 hours in a decompression tank before surfacing, with the mission being declared a success.

The next year, an all-female crew took control of the facility for a series of shorter missions that were partially paid for by NASA. The research was intended to help train astronauts for space. It was these women who paved the way for female astronauts to be included on future space missions.

The US government removed the actual habitat from the ocean decades ago, but if you strap on a snorkel mask and dive into the bay, you can still see the foundation pads in the seabed. They're solid evidence that science fiction isn't always make-believe after all.

MONTSERRAT, UK

SOUFRIÈRE HILLS VOLCANO

Life was peaceful on the small island of Montserrat, a British territory in the Caribbean. But on July 18, 1995, the Soufrière Hills volcano erupted and red-hot lava flowed across the island. The capital, Plymouth, was buried, as were many other towns and forests. Most of the island was left covered in ash. Two years later the volcano erupted again, destroying even more of the island. As a result, most of the residents left, but those who stayed found a way to use the volcanic ruin to their advantage. This island, frozen in ash, is now a tourist destination. Visitors can see rooftops and church steeples peek out from under solidified ash in Plymouth, or visit the Montserrat Volcano Observatory to learn about the volcano's lively past . . . and take a guess when the still-active Soufrière Hills will erupt again.

BEQUIA, ST VINCENT & THE GRENADINES

THE MOONHOLE

IN THE 1950S TOM AND Gladdi Johnston moved to Bequia and became fascinated by a local oddity called the Moonhole. A large natural rock archway, the Moonhole got its name because when the angle is just right, the archway frames the moon. The Johnstons spent so much time camping there that they decided to build a house in that very spot. They didn't have any experience building a house, but that didn't stop them.

Their dream house flowed in and out of nature. The floors were uneven, the walls constructed from rock, and everything else made of found objects like whalebone. Because it was so remote, the house didn't have running water; rainwater from the roofs was instead collected in cisterns. The original house is uninhabitable, with dangerous rocks falling in on its roof. Today you can only view the beautiful wreck from the sea.

ANTARCTICA

DECEPTION ISLAND

THIS ISLAND IN THE REMOTE South Shetland Islands archipelago is hiding more than a few secrets. Inside a collapsed volcanic crater is one of the world's safest natural harbors. But to get there, you must sail through a narrow break in the volcano's walls. This break has been known by a few names: Neptune's Bellows (because of the strong winds that blow through the passage), Dragon's Mouth, and Hell's Gates. Not exactly a cheerful welcome!

Whatever name it's given, once you're in, you'll find a horseshoe-shaped bay surrounded by black sand beaches. Chinstrap penguins toddle up and down the ash-covered snow and ice.

GIDDY UP
with these giant steel
horse heads **p96**

LONGITUDE
−60° / 0°

**IS THAT
A MIRAGE?**
No, it really *is*
a crystal clear
lagoon **p86**

PRAY IN A MOSQUE that's also the
world's largest mud-brick building **p94**

STAY BACK~
this island is completely covered in snakes **p85**

LAY OUT ON A BEACH . . .
in the middle of a field **p93**

DO YOU BELIEVE IN UFOS?
This town certainly does **p83**

Bonito, Brazil

GRUTA DO LAGO AZUL

Beneath a ceiling dripping with stalactites, a pool of crystalline turquoise water has gathered in this gorgeous grotto. It's one of the largest flooded cavities on the planet and more than 230ft (70m) deep. In 1992 a diving team explored those vast depths.

What did they discover? A treasure trove of pre-historic animal remains littering the grotto's floor, including the bones of saber-toothed tigers and giant sloths.

Varginha, Brazil

NAVE ESPACIAL DE VARGINHA

DO YOU BELIEVE IN UFOS?

The town of Varginha sure does. In 1996 locals swore they saw an unidentified flying object, and even an actual alien. The town was soon swarmed with UFO-seeking tourists. Businesses decided to get in on the action and started selling all sorts of alien-themed souvenirs. In 2001 the town needed to build a water tower, and what better shape to build it in than a flying saucer? Called "the Spaceship of Varginha," the tower looms 66ft (20m) above the town. It even lights up at night, bright enough to attract any lost UFOs that might be passing by.

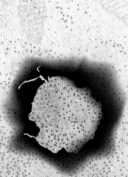

Alto Paraíso de Goiás, Brazil

VALE DA LUA

Vale da Lua translates to Moon Valley, which is the perfect name for this series of beautiful rock formations. Stretching along the southern edge of Parque Nacional da Chapada dos Veadeiros in Brazil, these formations were caused by fluvial abrasion—the pressure of sand and constantly flowing water. Over millions of years, water sculpted the area into what looks like a natural water park, but with sparkling quartz embedded in its stones. It's better than any lazy river you'll find.

BRAZIL

SNAKE ISLAND

IF YOU HATE SNAKES, this place is the stuff of nightmares. Ilha da Queimada Grande, off the coast of Brazil, is entirely populated by these slithering reptiles. Athough the island is tiny, there are several *thousand* snakes living there, which means you're in danger of stepping on a snake every square meter! And you definitely don't want to step on these snakes—their venom is so deadly it can melt human flesh.

It wasn't always this way. The island used to be attached to the mainland, but rising sea levels cut it off, stranding the snakes on their island habitat. Left alone, the snakes survived on a diet of birds and were able to multiply fast, developing lethal venom. It may be the most dangerous island on the planet but never fear: the island is off-limits to everyone except researchers and the military.

MARANHÃO, BRAZIL

PARQUE NACIONAL
DOS LENÇÓIS
MARANHENSES

ARE YOU DREAMING?

You'll think so seeing these mirage-like lagoons in the midst of towering sand dunes. Parque Nacional dos Lençóis Maranhenses in Brazil is a 598 sq mi (1,548 sq km) national treasure. With its crystal blue water shimmering against the bright white dunes, the lagoons seem to transcend reality. But dipping a toe into these refreshing pools of water would make anyone happy to be wide awake in this paradise.

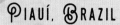

ROCK PAINTINGS OF PARQUE NACIONAL SERRA DA CAPIVARA

The red stone arches and bursts of greenery are remarkable enough at this national park and Unesco World Heritage site in Brazil. But take a stroll along the wooden walkways, and you'll see what's really special about this place. Some 40,000 prehistoric rock paintings decorate the cliffs. There's over 300 sites, and most of them date back to 30,000 to 50,000 BC! This art offers a glimpse into the life of South America's earliest human residents—first, hunter-gatherers and then later, farmers and pottery makers. Images on the walls represent animals, hunting scenes, and pictures of dancing figures. Inside one of the oldest sites are the remains of a 50,000-year-old hearth. You can only imagine that the paintings on the walls were the stories these ancient humans told around a fire.

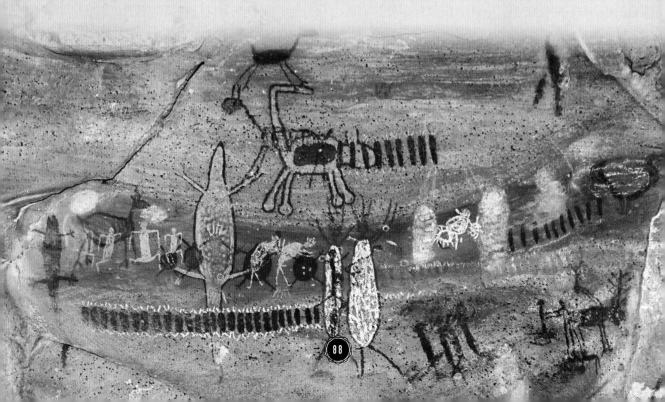

Near Dakar, Senegal
LAC ROSE

Not far from Senegal's sprawling capital, this shimmering lake glows like rose-colored glass.

What makes it pink? The lake has a really high salt content. That salty environment is ideal for the *Dunaliella salina* bacteria, which flourish there. They produce a red pigment in order to absorb light from the sun, giving the lake its vibrant color.

Apart from taking in the sights, you can come to the lake to relax too. Just like the Dead Sea in Jordan, you can float effortlessly on the surface. The salt will keep you buoyed up better than that giant swan floatie in your pool.

Senegal & Gambia

SENEGAMBIAN STONE CIRCLES

DEATH IS THE BIGGEST mystery . . . and these stone circles in Senegal and Gambia just add to the confusion! Up in the grasslands, rock pillars are arranged in over 1,000 circles around or near burial plots. The bones found inside the circles are laid out in elaborate patterns, but what those patterns mean is anyone's guess—archaeologists are still debating it! In fact, no one really knows who constructed the circles, or when. Such mystery adds to the magical feel, and may have you wondering if they're a gateway to another world. But to the local Gambians it's an ordinary, everyday sort of magic. Oftentimes they visit on their way to work to leave a stone atop one of the pillars. Then they'll take a moment to reflect or make a wish, and continue on with their day.

El Jadida, Morocco

CITÉ PORTUGAISE

BUILT IN THE 1500S, probably as an armory, this spectacular Moroccan building was then converted into a church and a cistern, or a place to store water. But the cistern has never been fully drained. A thin layer of water still covers the floor. When shafts of light shine through the ceiling, their reflections bounce off the water and dance on the stone columns and arches. The result is a play of light and shadow that's mesmerizing.

FEZ, MOROCCO
WATER CLOCK

From the street, this may look like a regular building, but it's actually a clock! Built in 1357, it was the home of the *muwaqqit*, or timekeeper. It was his vital job to give the correct times to call the Muslims in the city to prayer. He used the clock, which was a system of ropes and pulleys powered by the movement of water as it drained from a container. As the water level dipped, it pulled on the rope, opening a series of twelve doors. Each hour, a door would open and release a metal ball into a brass bowl positioned on a platform above the street. Passersby could tell the time by counting how many balls were displayed. While the clock may not be used to keep prayer time anymore, it's still a wonder to behold.

Near Llanes, Spain

PLAYA DE GULPIYURI

STANDING IN THE SOFT SAND
with the cool seawater washing over
your toes, you'd think you were on a
beach . . . except Playa de Gulpiyuri is
in the middle of a Spanish field.
This tiny body of water is
actually a flooded sink-
hole, framed by dramatic
limestone crags. A 330ft (101m) tunnel
runs beneath the ground all the way to
the Cantabrian Sea, which is where the
water comes from. You get the best of
both worlds: a gorgeous "beach" but no
chance of being swept out to sea!

DJENNÉ, MALI

GRANDE MOSQUÉE

AS THE NAME SUGGESTS, this mosque is exceptionally grand—and also the world's largest mud-brick building! But a structure made out of mud takes a lot of upkeep, and every year after the rainy season 4,000 local volunteers get to work restoring the mosque. Built in 1907, the site actually dates to 1280, when Djenné's 26th king, Koi Konboro, constructed the original mosque after his conversion to Islam. The mosque stood for over 500 years before it was abandoned to ruin by the warrior-king Cheikou Amadou in the early 1800s.

FALKIRK, SCOTLAND
THE KELPIES

THESE TOWERING STEEL horses look like they might rear up out of the earth. Andy Scott's glittering sculptures celebrate Scotland's waterways and industrial history. And while that may seem very modern, the folklore of the Kelpies goes way back. In ancient Scottish myth, kelpies are shape-shifting water creatures. They could take the forms of humans or horses . . . and often lured people to their doom. But fear not, these enormous horse heads have more in common with the gentle Clydesdale horses that pulled barges along Scotland's canals than with the fearsome water spirits they are named for.

BANDIAGARA ESCARPMENT, MALI

CLIFF DWELLINGS OF THE BANDIAGARA

Traveling through Dogon Country is like walking through the pages of a fantasy novel. The mud-and-rock structures here cling to the cliffs like precarious hobbit-holes. The isolation of the Dogon people isn't by accident. The steep cliffs and slopes of the Bandiagara Escarpment closes Dogon off from the rest of Mali . . . and therefore from invasion. That was a concern centuries ago when the dwellings were built, and is unfortunately still a fear today in Mali's uncertain political climate. But it's easy to forget the outside world as you wander among the elaborately carved doors and straw-roofed storehouses. The fairy-tale feel of the villages is part of what makes this one of West Africa's most impressive sites.

Koro, Mali

ANTOGO
FISHING FRENZY

AH, FISHING. SUCH A

peaceful and serene activity—but not in Koro. Though fishing is usually forbidden in this sacred lake, every year the village elders choose a day for the fishermen to gather at the water. The men jostle for position until the elders give a signal. Then they plunge into the water to grab as many fish as they can with their bare hands. It's a mad, crazy, mud-covered dash! Afterward they bring home their prizes for dinner.

ACCRA, GHANA
KANE KWEI COFFINS

SPEND ETERNITY INSIDE a huge wooden fish or a giant chicken head. At Kane Kwei Carpentry Workshop, no request is too bizarre. The business was started in the 1950s by carpenter Seth Kane Kwei, and now his son and grandson carry on the tradition of creating fantastical coffins. The coffins usually represent the lives of the people who are buried in them. A writer can be buried in a giant pen, or a musician in a wooden guitar. Some of the more unusual requests have been a cell phone, a hair dryer, and a beer bottle!

ORKNEY, SCOTLAND

ITALIAN CHAPEL

THE ORKNEY ISLANDS

may be cold and windswept, but the story of this chapel will warm your heart. Italian prisoners of WWII were brought to this island, and even though resources were limited because of the war, they were still able to create a beautiful place of worship using scrap metal. Serene murals decorate the walls and ceiling, and a rosy brick archway frames the altar. When Italy surrendered, the prisoners were granted their freedom. The chapel is now a symbol of reconciliation between two countries who were once at war with each other.

SAY HELLO to the "baby dragons" of the Postojna Caves **p126**

FOLLOW the shifting sand dunes of Råbjerg Mile **p120**

FOLLOW THE CURVE of a crooked forest **p125**

DANCE TO THE DRUMS of this voodoo ceremony **p109**

UNLOCK the secrets of the seed vault **p134**

IS IT HOT IN HERE? This gas crater has burned for 50 years **p156**

DO NOT ENTER~
this is the site of a major
nuclear disaster **p152**

LONGITUDE
0°/60°

SWIM UNDER
the waterfalls at
Plitvice Lakes
National Park **p128**

LIVE ON THE EDGE
for this spectacular vista **p105**

STEAL AWAY
to this cave with
the long-eared bats
p137

Savonnières, France

LES GROTTES PÉTRIFIANTES

ART TAKES TIME, AND that's especially true of the caves in the Loire Valley. Place any object (but maybe not one you're really attached to) in the cave's waters, and within a year it will be totally coated in limestone! The mineral-rich water drips down the walls of the cave, capturing anything in its path and covering it with a glistening coat.

The caves themselves are also a work of art. Like an underground goblin kingdom, there are grottos of dangling stalactites and all sorts of rock shapes that have taken centuries to form.

NEAR TYSSEDAL, NORWAY

TROLLTUNGA

If you've ever wondered what it's like to sit on a giant troll's tongue, this rock might give you an idea. A 12-hour hike out from the village of Skjeggedal brings you to this spectacular vista of sheer cliffs over water. Those who dare can balance on this outcrop for the ultimate photo.

ESBJERG, DENMARK

MAN MEETS THE SEA

THESE HUGE STATUES MIGHT look like something from your imagination, but these are real-life art installations by Svend Wiig Hansen. The stone men stand at 30ft (9m) tall, and will greet you as you sail into the harbor in Esbjerg. Hansen wanted the larger-than-life sculptures to capture the timeless relationship between humans and nature. Coming face-to-face with them at the seaside, it feels like you're being welcomed back to land.

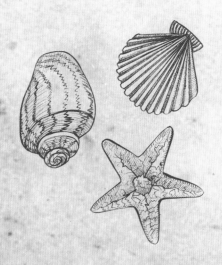

PARIS, FRANCE
CATACOMBES DE PARIS

AH, PARIS. CITY OF LIGHT, full of romance and . . . death? Below its lovely boulevards snakes a kingdom of the dead. Damp passageways that run beneath the city contain the bones of an estimated six million people! The problem began at least 250 years ago, when the population of Paris got too big for the cemeteries to handle. After a wall collapsed from the pressure of a mass grave, bodies were placed in what are now the catacombs.

Les Catacombes de Paris were also put to use by both sides during WWII. Both the Nazis and the French Resistance went underground. A room known as "Le Bunker" still sports signs in German forbidding smoking and talking.

Visitors should keep their wits about them. Some who go into the tunnels never come out! An 18th-century doorkeeper named Philibert Aspairt disappeared in the tunnels. His body was found 11 years later and had to be identified by the rusty keys on his belt. It's a grim place here for sure, but also filled with the history of an eternal city.

COVE, BENIN

EGUNGUN VOODOO CEREMONY

The drumming begins at dawn. People pour in from across the valley to the village of Cove. They're here for the Egungun Ceremony, which they believe will open a portal for the return of their dead ancestors.

Voodoo is a belief system at least 6,000 years old, and more than half of Benin's population practices it. Dancers for the annual Egungun Ceremony wear stunningly decorative costumes that completely hide the person within. As they dance to the drums, they open their souls and bodies to spirits. The ancestors can then look out of the dancers' eyes and see how their descendants are doing. Spectators call out favors of their ancestors, hoping for some help from the beyond.

The dancers twist and whirl as the drums get louder. But spectators must stay back—if they accidentally touch a dancer, it's believed they can get dragged into the spirit world. Witch doctors stay close in case they need to pull someone back to this world. In this dizzying mix of music, color, and spirituality, it's hard not to get swept away.

OSOGBO, NIGERIA
OSUN SACRED FOREST

This lush forest contains a meandering river and 40 shrines—many dedicated to Osun, the fertility goddess of the Yoruba religion. Archaeologists believe that people first moved to the grove 400 years ago and settled at this site near the river. But now these woods are the last remnants of primary high forest in southern Nigeria. Take a walk through the area and you might glimpse a sitatunga antelope or a troop of white-throated monkeys. Gorgeous religious sculptures and temples, both new and old, add to the power of this space.

HAUTERIVES, FRANCE
LE PALAIS IDÉAL

INSPIRATION CAN STRIKE

in the most unexpected places. One day in 1879, postman Ferdinand Cheval was walking along his mail route when he stepped on a pebble. Cheval picked it up, and an astonishingly ambitious idea was born. The postman decided to build a dreamy palace *entirely* from the unusual pebbles that he found along his 18-mile (29km) route! You can imagine

the patience it must've taken him to build his dream. Over the course of 33 years, Cheval created fantastical gargoyles, archways, stairs, elaborate columns, and turrets—all out of tiny stones. Next time you trip over a rock, don't be so quick to kick it out of the way.

THE ALPS, SWITZERLAND

TRIFTBRÜCKE

DON'T LOOK DOWN!

There's a sheer drop from the cliffs of Trift Gorge straight down to the turquoise waters of Lake Triftsee. But never fear. You're on the Triftbrücke, a feat of Swiss engineering that was built in 2009. Modeled after the three-rope bridges in Nepal, the Triftbrücke is considered one of the longest and highest pedestrian bridges in the Alps. Just fix your gaze to the stunning beauty of the Alps ahead of you and you'll make it safely across to the other side.

HAMBURG, GERMANY

MINIATUR WUNDERLAND

YOU'LL WISH YOU WERE miniature-sized just so you could jump in and wander this sprawling wonderland. The largest model railway in the world, Miniatur Wunderland has it all. From doll-sized buildings to sports stadiums with teeny-tiny people cheering on their champions, it's just like the real world, but condensed! The City of Hamburg is recreated down to the most minute detail. Miniatur Wunderland was started in 2000 and so far it's taken 760,000 hours to build. But it's not done yet! Big additions are planned, making its future not-so-tiny and bright.

Near Agadez, Niger

TREE OF TÉNÉRÉ

HERE STANDS THE SOLE surviving tree of the ancient Sahara forests. Well, sort of. The famous tree marked a critical water well for those crossing the brutal desert. It was the last tree standing here until 1973, when a truck driver knocked it down. Now a metal replica tree stands in the original tree's place—it's not quite the same, but it still serves as a symbol of hope in the heat of the desert.

SOUTH TYROL, ITALY

CAMPANILE DI CURON

AT FIRST, THIS LOOKS just like a regular lake . . . until you notice the bell tower rising eerily from its depths. The lake of Reschensee in Italy's South Tyrol was man-made in 1950. Three lakes were converted into one when a dam was constructed. Miles of farmland and dozens of homes were submerged, including a 14th-century church. But the water didn't rise high enough to cover the tall bell tower. When the water freezes, you can even walk out to the tower. There are about 64,000 churches in Italy, but this one may be the most unusual.

NEAR AGADEZ, NIGER

MEMORIAL TO UTA 772

THIS REMARKABLE MEMORIAL to UTA Flight 772 passengers ensures that those lost will be remembered forever. After the plane was bombed in September 1989, families of the deceased came together with 140 local Nigerians to construct the memorial. Formed out of black rock in the shape of a life-sized DC10 jet, the memorial points toward Paris, the final destination of the flight. One hundred and seventy broken mirrors dot the circumference to symbolize the victims, and one of the plane's wings rises up out of the sand dunes like a three-dimensional compass point. The memorial can even be seen from space. Type its name into Google Maps and you will see its striking shadow.

ROME, ITALY

VIA APPIA ANTICA

Europe's first superhighway was started in 312 BC by Appius Claudius Caecus, and finished in 190 BC. Via Appia Antica linked Rome with the southern port of Brindisi, making it an incredibly important roadway for the Romans. They called it the Queen of Roads, and looking at the cobblestone street today, you can understand why. Tall pine trees line each side. Lush fields extend back from the road, filled with ancient ruins and tucked-away villas.

But this beautiful road has its share of dark history. Spartacus and his army of 6,000 slave rebels were crucified along this road in 71 BC. Back in its heyday, wealthy Romans built huge mausoleums for their dead loved ones here. And in the early days of Christianity, followers of that religion were driven underground to bury their dead. Approximately 185 miles (298km) of subterranean burial chambers run beneath Via Appia Antica, reminding us that still waters—or in this case, roads—really do run deep.

LUANDA, ANGOLA

PALÁCIO DE FERRO

Who built this ornate yellow building and where it came from is anyone's guess. The Palácio de Ferro opened as a cultural center in 2016, but its history before that is a mystery—no official record of the building exists. Rumor has it that it was built for an exposition in France in the 1890s. Then it was taken down and put on a ship headed to Madagascar. This ship then drifted into the currents off the coast of Angola and was claimed by the Portuguese rulers of the colony there. Wherever it came from, it's a jewel in Luanda's crown.

NEAR SKAGEN, DENMARK
RÅBJERG MILE

The Råbjerg Mile just can't stay put. At 130ft (40m) high and with 140 million cubic ft (43 million cubic m) of sand, it's Denmark's largest sand dune. It's part of a conservation zone, but the dune keeps shifting up to 50ft (15m) every year.

In Denmark, shifting sands have driven people out of their homes and even swallowed up buildings. In the 1800s the Danish government began to buy sand dunes and plant trees to try to stabilize the sand. But when they bought the Råbjerg Mile in 1900, they decided to see what would happen if they just left it alone.

Their experiment backfired because leaving it alone now means that the dunes are seeping out of the conservation zone. But that doesn't seem to bother the birdwatchers and hikers who come here to enjoy its rebellious beauty.

ŽELÍZY, CZECH REPUBLIC

ŽELÍZY STONE DEVILS

HIKING THROUGH THE forested outskirts of Želízy, about 20mi (42km) north of the Czech Republic's capital, Prague, it's startling to see huge stone heads leer out at you. Created in the mid-1800s by Vaclav Levy, a sculptor known more for his work in churches than in forests, these "devil heads" are definitely much more hellish than heavenly. Worn down over time and covered in moss, they're even creepier to those hiking through the area nowadays than they must have been nearly 200 years ago.

ZADAR, CROATIA

SEA ORGAN

BENEATH A MARBLE staircase on the coast of Croatia hides a set of 35 pipes inside an underwater chamber. An invention by architect Nikola Bašić, the motion of the waves pushing seawater into the pipes makes music! The melodies change depending on weather conditions. Listening to this ocean's song, it's almost like Neptune and his chorus of mermaids are singing to you.

Near Sicily, Italy

STROMBOLI

THIS VERY LIVELY VOLCANO is a ferry journey away from the island of Sicily. It's so full of life that there has never been a time in human history when it wasn't actively spewing lava. Because of this, ancient sailors nicknamed it "Lighthouse of the Mediterranean," though perhaps you'd want to sail your ship guided by something a little less fiery!

Visitors can hike across the volcano's bare and ashen landscape. Smoking craters at the summit steadily hiss steam and occasionally spew jets of ash and lava. Molten rocks tumble down the slopes into the Mediterranean 3000ft (914m) below. On a clear day you can see all the way to Italy's mainland. Each magical step on this island volcano is a reminder that it's captured human imaginations for thousand of years.

NOWE CZARNOWO, POLAND

CROOKED FOREST

THIS EERIE FOREST IS a mystery. The C-shaped trees here look so unnatural you might wonder if witchcraft was responsible. Some say a heavy amount of snow bent the trees when they were still young. Others say tanks blasted through during a long-ago war and ruined their growth. But the most likely culprits were some inventive farmers. Trees shaped like this would've been very useful for building ships. Could it be that a clever farmer figured out how to make them grow this way? If so, no one is admitting to it, and the trees are keeping their secret to themselves.

POSTOJNA, SLOVENIA

POSTOJNA CAVES

Dragons are mythical beings . . . right? You may change your mind after reading about what lives in these caves. Here, ghostly amphibians swim in the underground waterways. When they were first discovered in the 17th century, everyone thought they were baby dragons! In fact, they're a newt-like species called olm or proteus. The caves around this area are the only place on earth where they live.

While they may not be dragons, these creatures are incredibly special: they can survive up to 10 years without food and they are completely blind. They navigate by feeling for slight electrical fields.

The little dragons have made the caves a famous destination for over 140 years. The ceilings drip with stalactites and limestone rises from beneath to form an underworld cathedral. But the olms are the stars of this attraction. Biologists have been studying their regenerative powers, hoping to find a key to cancer therapies. Who knows what other secrets these not-so-mythical creatures may be keeping?

CROATIA

PLITVICE LAKES NATIONAL PARK

In the lush beauty of this national park, it's hard to imagine its war-torn past. Waterfalls tumble into bright blue lakes. Butterflies flutter above the water. This stunning place was once a spiritual refuge, where it's said a monk lived in a grotto by the canyon's edge. But during the Balkan Wars of the 1990s, land mines dotted the park. The mines have been rooted out now, leaving a gorgeous landscape for everyone to enjoy. The lake system here is constantly renewing itself: as water washes over the rocks, barriers are formed and then eroded away. In 100 years Plitvice will look completely different from how it does today.

⊙ NAMIBIA

WILD HORSES
OF THE NAMIB DESERT

NO ONE KNOWS HOW THE wild horses got there. Are they descended from cavalry horses abandoned by the German Imperial Army in 1915? Were their ancestors shipwrecked here en route to Australia from Europe? Baron Captain Hans-Heinrich von Wolf had a castle a hundred miles from here in 1909, but his widow abandoned it after he was killed in WWI. Considering he owned thoroughbreds, were these horses let loose from there to the wilds of the desert? Whatever their origin, the sight of them racing across the vast, barren expanse is magical to behold.

VIENNA, AUSTRIA

HUNDERTWASSERHAUS

Artist Friedensreich Hundertwasser decided he was tired of all the boring, stately structures surrounding him in Vienna. He designed these fairy-tale apartments with leafy roofs and trees growing out from the windows, uneven floors, and a bright, unusual color wheel of blue, coral, and gold. Hundertwasser also decreed that anyone living in the building had the right to do whatever they wanted with the space outside their windows. He had fun with his design and wanted everyone else to have fun too. Talk about coloring outside the lines!

CENTRAL CEDERBERG, SOUTH AFRICA

WOLFBERG ARCH

YOU HAVE TO CRAWL, scramble, balance, and squeeze yourself through caverns to get to this natural wonder. The 4-hour hike to the Arch passes through the Wolfberg Cracks, a series of splits and fractures carved into the cliff face. Then it flattens into a majestically beautiful landscape . . . and little shade. The Wolfberg Arch is a natural formation here that seems as if it's sculpted out of the rock—totally worth every sore muscle when you lay your eyes on it.

BAJINA BAŠTA, SERBIA

DRINA RIVER HOUSE

THIS TINY HOUSE IS perched on a rock in the middle of Drina River. It was built in the 1960s by locals who dreamed of a blissful escape from the noisy world. Though the house has been rebuilt many times due to damage from flooding, it's still a beautiful place full of peace. Seeing this little sanctuary emerge from the mists—defying gravity atop its rocky base—could make anyone want to leave the world behind too.

JUODKRANTĖ, LITHUANIA
WITCHES' HILL

Don't worry: none of the witches and wizards here will hurt you. Over 70 wooden figures line this open-air sculpture garden, and they're both charming and creepy. There are totem poles topped with dragons, there's a chair carved with ancient faces, and a witch's-tongue slide in the playground. You might need to leave a trail of breadcrumbs to find your way out!

SVALBARD, NORWAY
GLOBAL SEED VAULT

WHOEVER DREAMED UP Norway's Global Seed Vault has definitely seen their share of disaster movies. This remote outpost in the Arctic houses crop seeds—enough so that if disaster strikes, humankind can rebuild (or replant, as it were).

There are around 1,700 seed outposts around the world, but this one provides the ultimate backup plan: 968,000 samples of about 4,000 plant species! They're all kept safe in little sealed bags in this far-flung station, which is halfway between Norway and the North Pole.

Seeds can only be reclaimed by the country that put them there. And based on its security systems, the Vault's creators were also watching James Bond movies. Not content that the location itself is secure, extreme safeguards were put in place against both natural and man-made disasters. The Vault was built to stand the test of time—and a zombie apocalypse.

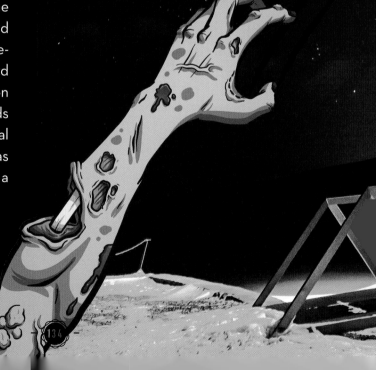

SLOVENSKÝ RAJ NATIONAL PARK, SLOVAKIA

DOBŠINSKÁ ICE CAVE

"DANGEROUS BEAUTY" are the words you could use to describe Slovenský Raj National Park. Beware of slipping into sinkholes, and watch out for bats fluttering around the limestone cliffs. But it's all the ice that will really make you shiver. Winter is forever in Dobšinská Ice Cave, situated so deep below the ground that warm air can't get in! This permanent freeze has allowed a huge amount of ice to cover the walls and ceiling, giving the cave its chilly name. The gleaming silvery walls, sparkling stalagmites, and thick columns of ice are fit for a Snow Queen's ballroom.

KALAHARI DESERT, BOTSWANA

GCWIHABA (DROTSKY'S) CAVE

Journey into one of the planet's last unknown corners at this cave in Botswana. Far away from any road or town, only the indigenous San people knew about it until recently. It's so well hidden that rumor has it a treasure was stashed here in the 1800s. It's unlikely you'll find any riches in this cave, though. Instead you'll encounter a cathedral of stalagmites and stalactites, long-eared bats, and complete isolation from the outside world.

Carpathian Mountains, Slovakia
WOODEN CHURCHES

DOTTED ALONG EASTERN Slovakia, these wooden churches appear like life-sized gingerbread houses in the middle of the countryside. The way they were constructed is just as magical—some of them were built completely without nails! From a church resembling a witch's hat to a whitewashed farmhouse look-alike, each church is unique. Getting inside is half the fun: most of the churches are locked, so visitors have to call the number tacked to the door and wait for the caretaker to let them in. It's worth the wait because inside these churches, you'll find gilded icons, intricate woodwork, and a rich history dating back centuries.

⑥ELOGRADCHIK, ⑥ULGARIA

KALETO FORTRESS

YOU COULD BE FORGIVEN for walking right past the Kaleto Fortress without seeing it. The citadel blends into the rocks on the northern slope of the Balkan Mountains. And this wasn't a mistake. The building's camouflage made it an ideal stronghold for over 200 years, starting in the late 1100s. From the ramparts, you would have been able to see an enemy army marching toward you across the hills. Today you can wander among the rocks and wonder at all the years of history they've seen.

STOB, BULGARIA

STOB PYRAMIDS

IT'S LIKE THESE SANDSTONE towers belong on another planet. Near Stob village, lush meadows end and orange dusty landscapes begin where these pyramids rise almost 40ft (12m) above jagged cliffs. Scientists say the otherworldly landscape was created by wind and snow. But local villagers tell a different story. Legend has it that during a wedding the best man kissed the groom's bride-to-be. The shock petrified the guests right then and there. Whether it's science or myth, this forest of stone is enthralling.

Near Šiauliai, Lithuania

HILL OF CROSSES

BACK IN THE 19TH CENTURY, area locals started laying crosses on this hill to honor loved ones killed in a rebellion. Over the years, what started as a small monument has grown to over 100,000 crosses! Soviet authorities bulldozed the site in 1961, but under cover of night, locals crept to the hill to lay more crosses. When the KGB (the Soviet state security committee) blocked the road and marked the area as quarantined, the faithful still kept coming, and the hill grew higher and higher.

When Lithuania finally won independence in 1990, the hill became a symbol of freedom and victory. People could lay their crosses openly, and so they do. The hill keeps growing every day. Talk about keeping the faith.

NIEU-BETHESDA, SOUTH AFRICA
OWL HOUSE

Great art can rise from the depths of despair, and the Owl House in South Africa is one such example. Helen Martins was unhappy in life, and poured her sadness into art, creating figures out of concrete. The figures come in both real and fantastical forms: mermaids, animals, farmers, religious scenes, and of course the trademark owl from which the house gets its name. They're brightly painted or decorated with colorful glass. In the face of bad fortune, Martins created something truly special.

Șinca, Romania

SINCA VECHE

ENTER THIS SACRED

Romanian dwelling and you'll join a long history of people who have come here to pray. The cave as we know it was established by monks in the 1700s, but archaeologists peg the cave's history back to 7,000 years ago. The cave caters to numerous religions, featuring a Chinese yin-yang symbol, a Jewish Star of David, and a Christian cross on the walls. Experiencing this fascinating place makes you see why it has inspired many years of worship.

MATOBO, ZIMBABWE

MATOBO NATIONAL PARK

ENTERING THIS WORLD

Heritage-listed park is like stepping into a dreamland. There are huge boulders that seem to teeter against one another, rainbow-colored lizards, ancient rock art, bright lichen, and soft vegetation. No wonder this place is sacred to the indigenous Ndebele people. The park is also home to the largest population of leopards in Africa. You may think you're dreaming, but this is the African wilderness at its most powerful and awe-inspiring.

BOTSWANA

KUBU ISLAND

THIS REMOTE CORNER OF the planet seems touched by a magic wand. Kubu Island rises from the world's largest network of salt flats. Twisted baobab trees are backed by a horizon that stretches on for forever. Though the landscape is dry now, five centuries ago there was a huge inland lake surrounding the island. Hippos wallowed in the shallows of that lake, and it's from them that Kubu gets its name: kubu means hippopotamus in the local Setswana language. It's easy to feel connected to the people who once lived here. There are stones and tools left here by ancient people, and not much has changed on Kubu Island since then.

Lopătari, Romania
LIVING FIRES

Watch your step as you pick your way across the plains of Lopătari. The land here is covered with fires that burst out from the soil! Natural gas smolders beneath the surface, fueling the flames that shoot out through cracks in the earth. When darkness falls, the expanse fills with orange and blue flames that look like they come from the underworld. But the Romanians have a more cheerful view of this place locally known as *Focul Viu*. They say the purifying fires protect wildlife and bring good fortune to those who visit.

PAMUKKALE, TURKEY

PAMUKKALE-HIERAPOLIS

THESE BASINS OF CLEAR blue water beckon you to kick off your shoes and wade in. The calm pools are contained in trays of calcium carbonate-turned-limestone called travertines. The water is the temperature of a perfect bath, which may explain why there has been a spa here since Greco-Roman times.

On the hillside above the water are the ancient ruins of the city of Hierapolis. A huge outdoor amphitheater is evidence of the wealthy community that once existed here. From the pools to the ruins, it's easy to imagine a day in the life of the ancient people who once lived here.

VIRUNGA MOUNTAINS, DEMOCRATIC REPUBLIC OF THE CONGO

NYIRAGONGO

What starts out as an ordinary hike through the forest soon turns into an extraordinary ascent to the mouth of a volcano. The vegetation thins out and the soft ground becomes a brittle field of black lava. Nyiragongo's last eruption was in 2002, and you can still see the remnants of that eruption the higher up the mountain you climb. Take shelter for the night right under the rim and watch the sky turn red from its fiery smoke. It's nature in its most magnificent—and terrifying—glory.

KASANKA NATIONAL PARK,
ZAMBIA

BAT
MIGRATION

Between October and December, 10 million golden fruit bats swarm into the tiny Mushitu swamp forest in Kasanka National Park. If you were to walk the forest floor during the day at this time of year, you'd be strolling underneath a massive canopy of sleeping bats. As the sun sets, the forest comes to life. From all around, the bats take flight, winging off into the dark.

UKRAINE

CHERNOBYL EXCLUSION ZONE

On April 26, 1986 a reactor inside the Chernobyl nuclear power plant exploded, creating the worst nuclear disaster in history. Today the zone has 10 times the normal amount of radiation, so you're not allowed to touch the vegetation. You would think nothing could survive this radioactive environment, but instead a strange sort of ecosystem has taken over. Trees twist through abandoned buildings. The grass reaches up to shoulder height. Birds sing from the trees and catfish swim in the river. An occasional bear lumbers through town.

Snapshots of life before the disaster are seen all over. The Ferris wheel and playground are rusted but still standing. Desks lay overturned in the desolate school, books strewn along the mossy floor. But Chernobyl isn't completely abandoned. A few elderly residents, called the grandmothers, or *babushkas*, returned here because they couldn't stand living anywhere else.

BAT, OMAN

BAT & AL AYN TOMBS

Everyone assumes that these brick structures are ancient tombs. The trouble is, none of them contain any bodies and there's no proof they ever did. The structures are 5000 years old and shaped like beehives. Perhaps they were temporary tombs, or maybe they were something different entirely—we may never know. What we do know is that the tombs form a striking silhouette against the mountain behind them. Perhaps it was the stark beauty of the rock face that inspired an ancient civilization to build them here, probably unaware that their origin would later remain a mystery.

ESFAHAN, IRAN

PIGEON TOWERS

Most of us want to avoid pigeon poop as much as possible. But not the builders of these towers in Iran. Their sole purpose was to collect pigeon excrement, and the more the better. Back when the towers were built in the 17th century, pigeon poop was used as fertilizer for farming. In order to keep their fields healthy, farmers needed the stuff, and often.

The solution was to build these towers. Known as dovecotes, they're specifically designed for pigeons to live and do their business in. The towers have hundreds of holes in them so pigeons could land, rest, and deposit their droppings. Since the poop was contained in one space, it was easier to gather without wasting a single precious drop. The method was so effective that thousands of these towers were built across Iran. They were also used in Egypt, Scotland, France, and the Baltics. But Iran's are probably the most impressive. The towers are actually quite pretty and stylish . . . if you don't know what is inside.

YAZD, IRAN

ZOROASTRIAN TOWERS OF SILENCE

No sound but the desert wind and the occasional cry of a vulture echo through the Towers of Silence. It's eerie for sure, and even more chilling when you know their purpose.

Built by the ancient practitioners of the religion Zoroastrianism, the Towers are where they came to bury their dead. Inside low stone houses, bodies were carefully washed and prepared. Then the dead were laid out in circles and left in the open for carrion birds to feed on. Once the bones were picked clean, they were lovingly placed inside the towers, known as ossuaries.

Zoroastrianism predates Judaism, Christianity, and Islam. Although the Towers of Silence are now empty and unused, Zoroastrianism is still practiced today in Iran, India, and across the rest of the world, though there are very few sects left that still observe this particular death ritual. The Towers of Silence now sit quietly, filled only with the ghosts of their past.

KARAKUM DESERT, TURKMENISTAN

DARVAZA GAS CRATER

This crater is nicknamed the "Door to Hell," and it's clear why—the boiling mud and fiery rock walls of this blazing pit create intense heat. Roughly the size of a soccer field, the crater is surrounded by a vast, bleak landscape. Though it might seem like a freak occurrence in nature, the crater is actually man-made. In 1971 Soviet engineers were hoping to strike oil in this spot, but their rig collapsed into a gas pocket. Worried that the methane gas would be dangerous, they set it on fire to burn the gas off. They thought it would burn out within a few weeks . . . but nearly 50 years later, it's still on fire.

SNACK ON BUGS at this
creepy-crawly market **p174**

CLIMB UP to a watchtower
on the Great Wall of China **p188**

CROSS A LIVING BRIDGE
made of tree roots **p165**

DISCOVER
a city under
the sea **p166**

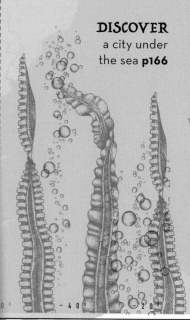

FIND the mythical golden egg at the top of a tower **p161**

LONGITUDE
60°/120°

VISIT the mysterious remains of an ancient civilization **p168**

PRAY at the temple where sacred rats scamper across the grounds **p162**

Hingol National Park, Pakistan

PRINCESS OF HOPE

RISING HIGH ABOVE THE sweeping deserts of Hingol National Park, the Princess of Hope gazes out as if she's surveying her kingdom.

The statue looks like it was carved by a skilled artisan, and it was—wind and rain. The powerful forces swirled together to create a natural wonder: a stone tower that resembles a woman in a flowing dress.

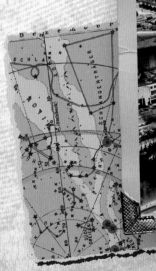

ASTANA, KAZAKHSTAN

BAYTEREK MONUMENT

This soaring tower looks futuristic, but was inspired by an ancient tale. According to Kazakh legend, a mythical bird laid a golden egg at the top of a sacred tree. The egg contained the secret to happiness but it was too high up in the tree for humans to reach. At Bayterek, however, the egg *can* be reached . . . by elevator! Travel up the white tree-shaped tower to the shimmering glass orb all the way at the top. Even if you don't find the secret to happiness there, you'll still experience stunning views of the city.

BIKANER, INDIA

KARNI MATA TEMPLE

Rats rule at Karni Mata. There are rats on the floors, rats on the stairwells, rats wriggling along handrails and skittering in every nook and cranny. But don't call an exterminator—the rats are meant to be here! They are thought to be the reincarnated children of Karni Mata, the Hindu warrior sage for whom the temple is dedicated. To enter the temple, you have to go barefoot, so if you don't want the critters scampering over your feet, you might want to stay outside. Inside, the walls echo with the squealing of the 25,000 rats that live there. Devoted pilgrims feed the animals out of their hands and kiss their tiny pink noses. Huge trays of milk and ceremonial food (called *prasad*) are laid out as offerings to the rats. It's considered a blessing to eat the food *after* the rats have already nibbled on it. Here they are not pests—they are sacred beings.

Mon State, Myanmar

KYAIKTIYO PAGODA

Giving new meaning to the phrase "defying gravity," this boulder stands 23ft (7m) tall as it leans toward the edge of its rocky perch. Only a tiny part of the stone touches the bedrock. Is it science or something more? Legend has it that a single strand of the Buddha's hair prevents the "Golden Rock" from toppling off the ledge.

That tale has made this one of Myanmar's most sacred pilgrimage sites. Every inch of the boulder has been lovingly painted with gold leaf.

A golden shrine, known as a stupa, sits on top like a crown. Buddhist pilgrims travel from all over just for the chance to put their own glittering mark on the rock.

But the journey here isn't easy. Pilgrims hike just under 7mi (11km) up a hard trail barefoot. Non-pilgrim visitors can keep their shoes on, but still ride up in rickety trucks along a bumpy road. The reward is a magical vista, especially at sunset.

KOLSAI LAKES NATIONAL PARK, KAZAKHSTAN

LAKE KAINDY

Lake Kaindy has a long and dramatic history. An earthquake in 1911 triggered a massive limestone landslide in these mountains, which in turn created a dam—and left this pristine lake. The water glows like jeweled turquoise, its vibrant color the product of limestone deposits. Spruce trees rise like spears out of the water, hinting at the submerged forest below. This serene place is a popular destination for scuba divers. The creation of the lake was a series of unfortunate events that ended up giving us something pretty special.

Mawsynram & Cherrapunjee, India

MEGHALAYA TREE BRIDGES

WHAT'S THE WETTEST PLACE on the planet? The two regions of Mawsynram and Cherrapunjee in the Indian state of Meghalaya compete for the title. But no matter which place wins, they're both famous for how they deal with their epic rainfalls. Locals have woven together walkways known as "living bridges" using the roots of rubber trees. Hollow tree trunks are positioned to help the roots grow. Once they are strong enough, the roots are braided into a bridge that can support the weight of 50 people! The bridges start to look like they grew naturally right out of the forest.

Yunnan Province, China

FUXIAN LAKE

For 1,750 years, Fuxian Lake kept its secret hidden. Then in 2001, divers discovered an ancient city covered in moss lying in ruins deep in the lake. Divers found mystical symbols carved into stone, animal-like masks, and ritual objects carved with the sun and moon. Scientists carbon-dated the ruins to approximately 260 AD, but the mystery of who lived here and how the city ended up underwater is still unknown. Perhaps it will be another 1,750 years before the lake gives up that secret too.

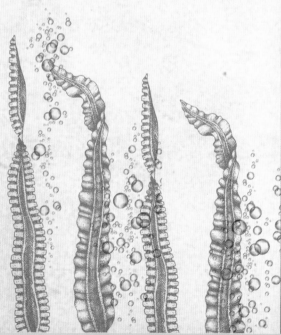

KARYAMUKTI, INDONESIA

GUNUNG PADANG

You would never know that this serene spot is the subject of a fierce archaeological fight. Ancient stone columns are scattered in this clearing in the lush hills of Cianjur, but how they got there is up for debate. Some say this is the site of a dormant volcano, and the rocks date back to 1200 BC. But others cling to the belief that the hunks of rock are much older . . . even up to 20,000 years old! Could these rocks be the ruins of a man-made pyramid? If so, it would mean this is the site of the most advanced ancient civilization *ever* discovered.

ZHANGYE, CHINA

ZHANGYE DANXIA NATIONAL GEOPARK

YOU WON'T HAVE TO RUN fast to chase a rainbow at this geopark. All the rainbows here are earthbound, and they never fade away. A masterpiece 20 million years in the making, these mountains shine with bands of bright color. Geological movement has pressed the sandstone into what looks like a layer cake dyed with several shades of food coloring.

Over time the sandstone has eroded into pillars and other shapes. The extreme desert heat split the rock, forming valleys of creeks and cliffs. During sunrise and sunset the hills blaze scarlet and gold. And after a rainstorm the colors are even brighter. The multicolored landscape is like a piece of artwork, painted by Mother Nature.

JOHOR BAHRU, MALAYSIA

ARULMIGU SRI RAJAKALIAMMAN

YOU'LL NEED SUNGLASSES in this sanctuary of glittering beads and glass. The story goes that while Guru Bhagawan Sittar sat wondering how to rebuild one of the city's oldest temples, he was struck in the eye by a ray of light. He discovered that the light came from the reflection of a glass artwork more than a mile away, which is when inspiration struck. He then created the temple using multi-colored beads and glass mosaics, and hung chandeliers to set light bouncing off every surface. Every single bead on the walls is engraved with a prayer, and the mosaics are made from more than 300,000 pieces of glass! It's sparkle taken to a whole new level.

Gurvan Saikhan National Park, Mongolia

YOLYN AM

YOU MIGHT THINK THAT ice in the middle of a desert is impossible, but that's exactly what you'll find in the Gobi Desert's Valley of the Vultures. Because of the shade in the canyon, ice persists here, even into the summer! The blue ice mixes with desert dust to form natural sculptures and steep crevasses. Unfortunately, due to climate change this beautiful mirage gets thinner by the year.

SINGAPORE

HAW PAR VILLA

In this surreal sculpture garden, over a thousand statues painted in vivid, glossy colors populate the garden. Some are nightmarish: a crab with a man's head or a girl with a snail's body. Others are dreamy: magnificent dragons and uplifting scenes of meditation. This introduction to the world of Chinese religion and mythology was built by brothers Aw Boon Haw and Aw Boon Par. They wanted to portray the idea of traditional Chinese moral values: do good deeds and you'll be rewarded, but do bad deeds and you'll be punished. The whimsical statues capture these important values of Buddhism and other Chinese religions.

NEAR SIEM REAP, CAMBODIA
KBAL SPEAN

The rushing water here can't hide the site's real draw: carvings of Hindu gods above and below the waterways. Vishnu reclines with his wife Lakshmi by his feet. Brahma sits regally on a lotus flower. A waterfall tumbles over monkey-headed Hanuman. It's believed that hermits sculpted the images as early as the 10th century.

To get here, you've got to make your way through the forest, hanging onto branches and tree roots to get uphill. You can miss a lot of the carvings because many are hidden by overgrown trees and waterfalls. But once here, you'll want to explore every nook and cranny of this hidden wonder.

SIEM REAP, CAMBODIA

CREEPY-CRAWLY
MARKET

HERE'S SOMETHING YOUR school cafeteria probably doesn't have on the menu: bugs. At the Creepy-Crawly Market, these critters are the only items available, but you can get any kind of bug imaginable!

The market moves every day to a different location in the city of Siem Reap. Here you can try pretty much anything that can be found under a rock: crickets, water bugs, spiders, and moth larvae. You can have them served raw, or fried in peanut oil for a crispy crunchy texture!

You may think that eating bugs is totally gross, but anthropologists believe that bugs were a staple of our diet some 10,000 years ago. You never know, one day you may find that you have a taste for tarantulas.

CHRISTMAS ISLAND, AUSTRALIA

RED CRAB MIGRATION

AT THE START OF THE rainy season, one of nature's most striking and sudden events takes place here. Tasting the first drops of rain, countless bright red crabs crawl out from underground burrows. Creeping sideways, they make their way to the beach 5mi (8km) away. Pretty soon, the slow trickle of crabs becomes a tide of millions, all scuttling to the sea.

What's their rush? They've gotta find their soulmate! Propelled by instinct, these little creatures stick to a tight schedule. They must migrate, burrow, woo, and mate by the turn of the high tide of the last quarter moon. Then the females shimmy into the waves, laying eggs into the water.

Local rangers patrol the streets with plastic rakes, scooping the critters out of harm's way from bikes, cars, and trucks. But dodging traffic isn't the worst of it. The tough little crabs must scale steep cliffs, scuttle over jagged rocks, and fight off hordes of angry yellow ants. With all these dangers, you can understand just how impressive their ritual is.

CHRISTMAS ISLAND, AUSTRALIA
THE GROTTO

To get to this cove you'll need to follow a narrow path along the sea, with only tropical birds for companions. Then you'll make a rocky climb down to a cave in the cliff wall. You'll hear the water before you see it, but eventually you'll come to a shallow pool of crystalline water.

The water of the Grotto shines bright turquoise, and overhead, stalactites dangle from the roof of the cave.

Locals have come up with a system to alert visitors of new arrivals. Leave your towel visible on the path and you'll hear a "Coo-eee!" if someone else approaches for a swim. The Grotto is to be enjoyed and shared by all.

NEAR HOI AN, VIETNAM

MY SON

BENEATH CAT'S TOOTH

Mountain lie the ruins of the ancient Champa kingdom, which thrived here from the 4th to the 13th century. Its kings and queens are buried at My Son, where 18 temples dedicated to the god Shiva still stand. Though nature has been slowly taking over the site, you can still see carvings of Hindu legends on the buildings. The kingdom was largely forgotten until 1898, when it was rediscovered by French scholars. The crumbling temples were restored in the 1930s, but during the Vietnam War, the site suffered extensive damage during a single week of bombings by the US. It's still standing, though—resilient even through war.

SIBERIA, RUSSIA
OLKHON ISLAND

I f the name Siberia makes you think of a bleak landscape of ice and snow, think again. This sun-warmed island of Olkhon is a peaceful, beautiful place on Lake Baikal. It is the home to the Buryats: indigenous people who believe the island to be a spiritual place. In the thick forest on the northern side of the island, every rock and oddly shaped tree is hung with a colorful cloth. This marks the place as an *oboo*, or home to a kindly spirit. Each natural landmark on the island has a special significance to the Buryats. To them, it makes sense that their benevolent spirits chose this welcoming island as their home.

Near Da Nang, Vietnam

AM PHU CAVE

Decorated to represent the Buddhist ideas of purgatory and hell, this cave carries a harsh moral message about what happens if you give in to evil. The sunlit top of Thuy Son, the "marble mountain" in which the cave is located, represents the heavens. From there, you descend down 10 levels, each painted with vivid scenes of gruesome punishment for evildoing. After this frightening trip, you can climb a steep staircase back up to the light. You'll definitely behave after having this taste of hell!

DALAT, VIETNAM
HANG NGA
GUESTHOUSE

IT'S NOT HARD TO see why this little hotel is nicknamed Crazy House. Architect and owner Mrs. Dang Viet Nga was inspired by the surreal architecture of Antoni Gaudí, and from the outside the place looks like a melted candle. But Crazy House is different from every angle. On one side, windows shaped like eyes stare at you, and warped walls seem to drip multicolored candle wax. On the other side, traditional Vietnamese designs soar above the eaves. Inside, sculpted jungle vines run along the walls and beds are nestled into fairytale nooks. Sounds confusing? That's kind of the point. Mrs. Nga wanted her guests to feel free when they stay the night.

WESTERN AUSTRALIA
CAPE LEEUWIN LIGHTHOUSE

At the most southwesterly point in Australia stands this lighthouse built in 1895. It has the honor of watching over not one but *two* oceans. To the south lie the cold waters of the Southern Ocean, rolling in from Antarctica. To the west are the warmer waves of the Indian Ocean, linking Australia to Africa. This spot marks exactly where the two oceans meet. And when conditions are just right, you can actually see offshore a clear line where the two oceans touch.

Near Magelang, Indonesia

GEREJA AYAM

In 1990 Daniel Alamsjah felt a divine calling to build a house of worship for all faiths. He decided to construct it in the shape of a dove, the everlasting symbol of peace. If you tilt your head and use your imagination, it *could* look like a dove. But the crown on the top of its head and the open red beak definitely make it look more like a rooster. Unfortunately the building was never finished, and the place was abandoned in 2000.

Now it's been downgraded from both a dove and a rooster, and is just referred to as the "Chicken Church." Moss covers the outside, like green feathers. The tail is crumbling and sections are covered in graffiti. The building has decayed so much that it's in danger of collapse. Perhaps soon this dove will fly away to make its nest somewhere else.

WESTERN AUSTRALIA

PRINCIPALITY OF HUTT RIVER

IF YOU'RE MIFFED THAT YOU weren't born into royalty, never fear. You can just declare yourself prince or princess of whatever piece of land you live on, like Leonard George Casley did in 1970. Angry at the Australian government over what he considered unfair agricultural laws, Casley pronounced himself Prince Leonard and his farm the Principality of Hutt River.

The micronation is 29 sq mi (75 sq km) and has a population of 23. Though it's not recognized by Australia, the Principality has its own currency, flag, bill of rights, and national anthem. Visitors (and there are a lot of them) have to get their passports stamped at the government offices in the capital city of Nain in order to be allowed inside its tiny borders. You can visit an impressive art museum and a miniature golf course used by the royal family, or picnic and camp overnight by the Hutt River. And don't forget to trade your Australian dollars for Hutt River currency! It may be useless everywhere else, but its rarity makes it a great collector's item.

BEIJING, CHINA

CHAIRMAN MAO MEMORIAL HALL

Thousands of people visit the preserved body of Mao Zedong and his final resting place in Beijing's Tiananmen Square. The Chairman of the Communist Party of China died in 1976 and his embalmed body has lain in state ever since. People line up to lay a marigold, a popular offering, on the tomb. The body is behind glass, and in the bustling environment, visitors tend to only catch a glimpse of this founding father of modern China.

Near Beijing, China

ZHENGBEI TOWER

Within the wonder that is the Great Wall of China, there is a forgotten stretch of the wall you can explore. If you break away from the better-known sections, you can wander off to the quiet village of Xizhazi. Climb up an ordinary path between cornfields and farmhouses. Pass sleepy dogs and ramshackle chicken coops. Hike through the woods until you get to a wall of brick and white stone.

Pick your way up a haphazard staircase, and you'll be inside a Ming Dynasty watchtower. The world spreads out below you from this high-up perch. The mountains to the west rise and fall like a roller coaster. From the upper battlements of the Zhengbei Tower, you can imagine yourself as a warrior long ago, your bow and arrow pointed down at any enemy who dared to attack.

Though this far-flung part of the wall is crumbling and overgrown, you can still picture what it must've been like hundreds of years ago. This Great Wall saw wars start and end, empires rise and fall.

ZHEJIANG PROVINCE, CHINA
LONGYOU CAVES

FOR AGES, PEOPLE THOUGHT

Longyou's ponds were bottomless. But in 1992 some curious locals decided to figure out just how deep the ponds really were, and discovered more than they bargained for: an elaborate system of man-made caves.

Stretching out over 300,000 sq ft (28,000 sq m), there are 36 grottos. Every chamber is decorated with the exact same pattern of straight lines. Fish, birds, animals, and scenes of ordinary ancient life are also chiseled into the sandstone. The water was pumped out of the caves, and now the sun spills in from the open skylights, illuminating this wondrous underground discovery.

Scientists can't pinpoint when the caves were built, but their best guess is around 200 BC. Who created the carvings and why is a mystery. One theory posits the caves were a re-creation of the constellations that their builders saw in the sky above them. Whatever the truth may be, the Longyou Caves are keeping quiet about it, for now.

Western Australia
GNOMESVILLE

Once upon a time, a garden gnome appeared in the hollow of a tree at this roundabout. But the gnome was lonely. Sympathetic townspeople placed other garden gnomes next to him so he would have some company. And thus, a village—and a major tourist attraction—was born. Gnomesville has grown to a population of at least 5,000 gnomes! The gnomes come from all over the world, as visitors flock here to bring their own garden gnomes to this sanctuary. There are gnomes of every design: partying gnomes, plane-flying gnomes, and even a gnome sitting on a toilet. If the gnomes misbehave, they go to the fenced-in "Gnome Detention Center." Signs around Gnomesville proclaim, "Gnome Wasn't Built In A Day" or "Better Gnomes & Gardens." If you've got a garden gnome, why not consider relocating it to Gnomesville? After all, there's no place like Gnome.

SHORT ON CASH?
Trade these 12-foot-high stones instead **p209**

LOOK UP at a cliff of hanging coffins **p196**

KEEP YOUR DISTANCE~
these geysers spew volcanic gas **p231**

TOUR
a submarine from a failed spy mission **p206**

DIP INTO a thermal bath . . .
alongside Japanese snow monkeys **p210**

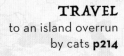

WALK AMONG
a ghost town covered
in vines **p199**

TRAVEL
to an island overrun
by cats **p214**

LONGITUDE
120°/180°

**SNEAK
A PEEK**
at these
neon slugs
p216

VISIT an abandoned
island town **p207**

WESTERN AUSTRALIA
LAKE HILLIER

IF YOU WERE GOING TO draw a body of water, you'd probably use your blue pencil—unless you're drawing Lake Hillier, which is bright, bright pink! No one knows why this body of water, so close to the blue Southern Ocean, is the color of bubble gum. The rosy hue may be caused by the same type of bacteria that makes other lakes pink, though this has never been confirmed. One thing is for sure: the water from Lake Hillier stays pink even when you scoop it into a bottle. You can't visit the lake since it's part of a restricted wilderness preserve, but you can take a helicopter tour over it for a view of all its pink glory.

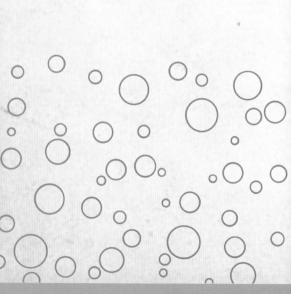

SAGADA, PHILIPPINES

ECHO VALLEY HANGING COFFINS

LOOKING UP AT THE CLIFFS on the mountainous island of Luzon, you'll find coffins hanging down the rock face. The island is populated with the indigenous Igorot people, and their open-air cemeteries are a blend of spiritual and practical. The Igorot believe that the higher up the coffins are, the closer they are to the spirits of their ancestors. Igorot elders actually build their own coffins, and after they die, their bodies are smoked and wrapped tightly in cloth. They are then carried to the cliffs in a procession of honor and stakes are driven into the cliff to hold the coffins in place. The practical side of the hanging coffins is that they are kept safe from scavenging animals, floods, and—in rougher times—grave robbers.

The practice of hanging coffins is slowly dying out as the older population of Igorots passes on. But these unique cemeteries are likely to endure for generations to come.

Near Shanghai, China

UPSIDE-DOWN HOUSE

Some days you can feel like your life is upside-down. But if you're this house, it really is. From the outside, it looks like a giant picked up this Scandinavian-style home and dumped it on its head. Inside, things get wackier. All the tables, chairs, sofas, and toys hang on the ceiling (which is really the floor) above your head. Even the toilet is upside-down. It's definitely dizzying, but what's cooler than actually dancing on a ceiling?

YILAN, TAIWAN

BENEFICIAL MICROBES MUSEUM

Put away your hand sanitizer. Here, bacteria are celebrated. The goal of this Taiwanese museum is to help people understand all the good that bacteria do for us. It teaches people about friendly microorganisms and which bacteria are harmful. There's a workshop on fungus and skin-care experiments. Even germophobes will surely leave with a newfound respect for the bacteria soldiers that protect our bodies every day.

SHENGSHAN ISLAND, CHINA

HOUTOUWAN

HALFWAY BETWEEN CREEPY and magical is this island ghost town. A once-busy fishing village, the people drifted away over the years to find jobs in the big cities. Now there are only a few elderly residents left, and nature has taken over the town. Peek into a crumbling house and you'll see furniture coated in dust. Try to climb a staircase and you'll have to fight through overgrown vines. The desolation might be a little eerie, but the greenery that has swallowed up much of the village is what makes this place so special.

Taichung, Taiwan

RAINBOW VILLAGE

FEARFUL THAT HIS FADING village would be destroyed, former soldier Huang Yung-Fu picked up a paintbrush and set to work. He covered every surface with colorful paintings of birds, flowers, and Chinese figures. Nicknamed "Grandpa Rainbow," his efforts paid off: locals saved the town from demolition, and now it's on its way to being designated a cultural landmark.

JEJU ISLAND, SOUTH KOREA
HAENYEO

DON'T BELIEVE IN MERMAIDS? You may change your mind after meeting the women divers of Jeju Island in South Korea. Known as "Korea's mermaids," the haenyeo dive so deep into the cold ocean that they seem to defy the laws of nature . . . or at least human lung capacity! The diving tradition is passed down from mother to daughter. They start training young so that by the time they're ready to dive, they can hold their breath for way longer than your swimming instructor thought possible.

While mining treasure such as octopus, abalone, and sea urchins is their mission, they've also been witness to the changing ocean. Because of pollution, the abalone they seek is becoming increasingly rare. And the tradition is dying out. Many daughters choose to leave Jeju to seek their fortunes in the big city.

IRIOMOTE ISLAND, JAPAN

STAR-SAND BEACHES

On a few remote beaches in Japan, you can hold the stars in your hand. Legend has it that the star-shaped grains of sand are the children of the stars in the sky. Really, they're the exoskeletons of tiny sea creatures. The creatures wash up on shore by the millions, especially after sea storms. Sadly, overeager merchants are scooping up the unique sand and bottling it to sell to tourists faster than the sand can replenish itself. So visitors should remember to admire the stars in the palms of their hands, and then let them go so the next visitors are able to hold the stars too.

CHINA & NORTH KOREA

HEAVEN LAKE

This bright blue lake does indeed look heavenly, as its name suggests. Situated at the top of Mt Paektu, it's located in the caldera of a volcano, which is a hollow crater created by large eruptions of magma over a short period of time. And though this volcano on the Chinese and North Korean border is still active, the lake is peaceful. But rumors of what lies beneath are not so serene. Since 1903 there have been sightings of the "Lake Tianchi Monster." In 2007 a local filmmaker shot a grainy film that appears to show several seal-like, finned creatures frolicking in the water. Perhaps Scotland's Loch Ness Monster has an Asian cousin.

SOUTH AUSTRALIA
COOBER PEDY

Coober Pedy is no ordinary town. It is, quite literally, a town beneath your feet. What drove the people underground? Coober Pedy is the world's largest supplier of opal stones. Deep shafts lead down to mines where the gemstones are collected. The majority of residents work under the ground and live in man-made caves dug into the hillsides. The dugouts maintain a comfortable temperature year-round, unlike the sweltering outback weather aboveground. Homes, churches, and stores are all carved out beneath the earth.

But the biggest attraction is actually aboveground: a grassless golf course. The course is all dirt except for a little piece of artificial turf that golfers carry around with them to tee off from. And for some who find the daytime heat too much to handle, you can play golf at night with a glow-in-the-dark ball. This surreal landscape is the one golf club where "Keep Off The Grass" signs aren't needed!

GANGNEUNG, SOUTH KOREA

NORTH KOREAN SUBMARINE

Undercover meant underwater on this North Korean submarine. It carried 26 North Korean spies into South Korean waters in the fall of 1996. Their mission was to gather information about South Korea's navy, then return to the submarine and glide away underwater without ever being discovered. This didn't quite go as planned. The submarine ran aground and the crew could not free the boat. They burned all the secret documents onboard and fled back to North Korea on foot. Only one of them possibly made it back: the others were all captured. And the submarine is still stuck in the same spot where the spies left it. Now you can visit the spy sub and creep through rusting metal corridors in Gangneung Unification Park. There's even scorch marks on the wall from when the sub's commander destroyed their secrets.

ⓃNAGASAKI, ⒿAPAN

HASHIMA

YOU'VE HEARD OF GHOST towns, but have you heard of a ghost island? That's exactly what Hashima is. As you wander past tumbledown buildings and alleyways covered with vines, it's hard to believe that this was once the most densely populated place in all of Japan.

Hashima was owned by a coal company, and the island bustled with workers and their families. When the mine closed down in 1974, it took just *four* months for the island to become completely abandoned. Now empty schools, clinics, and temples sit covered in dust. Iron gates rust off their hinges, and greenery has taken over the city.

Hashima was nicknamed Battleship Island because the silhouette it made against the water looked like that of a ship. Surrounded by the bleak, sun-bleached buildings, you might think that you're staring at the ruins of an ancient city. It's hard to believe that people left Hashima behind only 45 years ago.

NARA, JAPAN

NARA PARK

WE OFTEN THINK OF

deer as shy animals, but that's not true of the sika deer that roam the town of Nara. Legend has it that a mythical god rode into town on a white deer in the 8th century, and ever since then, deer have ruled the roost. The animals are considered treasures, and they're pretty much allowed to do anything here. They'll wander through stores, restaurants, and even some residents' houses! They don't hold back about asking for food, either. The deer will come right up to you and head-butt you until you feed them. If you do feed them, they are rumored to reward you by bowing in gratitude. They may not say "please" but at least they can show their "thank you."

⦿YAP, ⦿MICRONESIA

RAI STONES

WHEN YOU THINK OF buying something, you think of using cash or card—not *giant* limestone wheels. The stones measure up to 12ft (4m) high and can weigh 4 tons (3.6 metric tons). The curious thing is that the limestone doesn't actually come from this island. Legend has it that about 500 years ago a navigator landed in Palau, 250mi (402km) away. He traded his goods for limestone there, carved the stones into donut-shaped discs, and brought them back to Yap. The island has been using them as currency ever since. But how the heck do the people of Yap carry around these stones every time they want to purchase something? The answer is, they don't. The stones rarely move. Ownership—and the transfer of it—is simply recorded whenever there's a transaction.

JOSHINETSU KOGEN NATIONAL PARK, JAPAN

JIGOKUDANI MONKEY PARK

MONKEYS DO HAVE A

lot of human habits . . . including soaking in a nice hot bath. Japanese snow monkeys like to warm up at these hot springs, particularly during the coldest months of the year. The baths are open to the human public as well. People can step into the steaming water and end up sharing their bath with these sweet red-faced monkeys, who have also been caught at another familiar human activity: having a snowball fight!

NEAR LYNDOCH, SOUTH AUSTRALIA

WHISPERING WALL

STANDING TALL AT 118FT (36m), the curved concrete dam of Barossa Reservoir is pretty impressive on its own. But what makes it even more extraordinary is its "parabola effect." This effect makes it so that the softest whisper from far away can be heard. If you stand on one side of the dam, and have a friend stand on the other side 460ft (140m) away, you can whisper secrets to each other and it'll sound like your friend is speaking directly into your ear! Local legend has it that the effect was discovered when one of the dam's construction supervisors heard his workers gossiping about him. He fired them from the opposite side of the dam without even having to raise his voice.

WESTERN AUSTRALIA

LAKE BALLARD

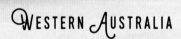

Shimmering under the outback sun is this salt lake. It appears like a mirage in the middle of a barren landscape, but it's only half the attraction. If you follow a set of deep-set tracks to the lake, you'll see 51 tall metal statues along the way. It's the world's largest outdoor art gallery, created by Antony Gormley. The sculptures represent the 51 residents of the nearest town, Menzies. Walking in and out of cloud shadows, your eyes will trick you. Is the lake right in front of you or still a good distance away? The eerie figures aren't telling.

TASHIROJIMA, JAPAN

CAT ISLAND

CAT LOVERS, REJOICE!

There is an entire island devoted to your favorite feline friend. On Tashirojima Island, cats outnumber people six to one. They're believed to be lucky, and keeping them as pets is considered bad taste. So the wild cats roam the island as they please. But don't worry. Taking care of the cats is also thought to bring good fortune, and so these cats are *very* well taken care of.

Tashirojima was made rich by silk and fishing over the centuries, and the cats were a big part of both. Cats were encouraged to chase mice away from silkworms, keeping the worms safe to spin their silk. Later, fishermen kept the cats happy by feeding them from their daily haul. Now the human population of the island is dwindling, and the cats are taking over, so there's plenty of room for you to move in and live out your ultimate cat-crazy dream.

MELBOURNE, AUSTRALIA

COW UP A TREE SCULPTURE

I t isn't every day you see a cow up a tree. But artist John Kelly was inspired to create an art sculpture based on two Australian themes: flooding and camouflage cows. Why are those themes Australian? Floods are a common occurrence in this part of Australia. As for camouflage cows, well, that's known to *not* be a common find. During WWII, artist William Dobell built life-sized papier-mâché cows and moved them around airfields, thinking that they would distract Japanese pilots. Spoiler alert: they didn't.

Inspired by the crafted cows, as well as the theme of flooding, Kelly came up with this bizarre sculpture. It's a cow that doesn't really look like a cow, stuck up in a tree. Because obviously that's where a cow would wind up during a flood, right? Real cows don't climb trees . . . but maybe papier-mâché ones do.

NEW SOUTH WALES, AUSTRALIA

GIANT PINK SLUGS OF MT KAPUTAR

On a remote peak 4,885ft (1,500m) above sea level live some vividly colored little creatures. This is the only place in the world where you can find them. They are bright neon slugs! The slugs come in various shapes and colors. Some are as long as a cucumber and hot pink, while others are triangular and bright red. After it rains, these guys crawl out from their underground lairs to feast on lichen and tree moss. They live in the remains of an extinct volcano, which was active 18 million years ago. Have the slugs been around that long? Scientists aren't sure. However long they've existed, their dazzling colors are captivating visitors who don't mind getting the creepy-crawlies.

KAMCHATKA PENINSULA, RUSSIA

VALLEY OF GEYSERS

JOURNEYING TO THE Kamchatka Peninsula on Russia's far-flung eastern reaches is like entering another planet. The five-mile (8km) valley stretches toward Japan, and is fed by the mega-heat of the Kikhpinych stratovolcano, a volcano that's made up of alternate layers of lava and ash. Not only that: the Valley of Geysers looks like it's smoking. But it's not fire—it's steam puffing into the cold air. Along one narrow creek, the volcanic gases are so thick that they can kill animals and birds that get too close.

New South Wales, Australia

SS AYRFIELD

IT'S HARD TO RECOGNIZE that this floating island is actually a ship. The SS *Ayrfield* was built in 1911 and played an important role in WWII, delivering supplies to US troops stationed in the Pacific. It was retired from service in 1972 and sent to Homebush Bay to be broken up for parts. Instead it was left to languish on the water. Over the last 50 years, the ship has been completely taken over by nature, so much so that now an entire forest has grown aboard the ship! You can barely see the rusting body beneath the greenery. Eventually the mangroves will pull the ship apart at its seams. Not even a sturdy ship that survived a war can survive Mother Nature.

GRANDE TERRE, NEW CALEDONIA

HEART OF VOH

THE MANGROVE TREES THAT grow on New Caledonia's main island of Grande Terre must really love each other. Over the last two centuries, the mangrove swamp has naturally grown in the shape of a perfect heart that can be viewed from the air. Visitors in the mood for romance can take an ultralight aircraft for a flyover. The flight gives new meaning to the phrase "love is in the air."

HIDEAWAY ISLAND, VANUATU

UNDERWATER POST OFFICE

Did you know it's possible to mail a letter while scuba diving? The mailbox is stationed underwater in a marine sanctuary just off the shore of Hideaway Island. You can swim 10ft (3m) down and drop off a waterproof postcard marked with an inkless stamp. Every day, a scuba-diving postal worker collects the mail. Dogs don't bother these postal workers, but they've got a slightly bigger worry—having to fend off curious reef sharks!

PENTECOST ISLAND, VANUATU

LAND DIVERS OF PENTECOST ISLAND

IF YOU THINK BUNGEE

jumping is wild, you haven't heard of the people who invented it. The young men of Pentecost Island start by building wooden towers in April each year. They carefully measure platform heights and test the sturdiness of the trees and vines they use. When the structures are ready, the young men climb to the top, tie a liana vine around each of their ankles, and jump. All that careful measuring means that each jumper's head barely grazes the ground!

These young men are called land divers, and this ancient ritual has been going on for centuries. Participants believe it ensures a fruitful yam harvest.

DUNEDIN, NEW ZEALAND

BALDWIN STREET

Meet the world's steepest drivable street, according to the *Guinness Book of World Records*. Baldwin Street is only 1,150ft (351m) long but has a 19-degree gradient at its steepest point. If you take a picture at a certain angle, all the houses look like they're sinking into the ground!

Hokitika, New Zealand

WILDFOODS FESTIVAL

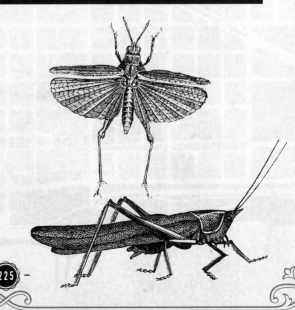

In the mood for some earthworm sushi? How about pickled grubs or chocolate-covered beetles? You can find all that and more at this annual food festival in New Zealand. Munch on live grasshoppers, cockroaches served in cups of pink jelly, or mountain oysters (another name for sheep testicles). Only those with strong stomachs need apply.

GIBBS FARM, NEW ZEALAND

ELECTRUM

ART AND SCIENCE COLLIDE in Electrum, a mind-blowing sculpture by Eric Orr and Greg Leyh. It's shaped like a four-story-high lollipop, but you definitely can't lick it. Over 3 million volts of electricity are harnessed in Electrum, the world's largest Tesla coil.

In 1891 Nikola Tesla invented his coil, which sucks electrons from the air and gives off massive voltage. Streams of electricity fly off the coil in crackling arcs like lightning. Watching a Tesla coil in action is like watching something out of a mad scientist movie. At Electrum, it takes that image one step further. Look deep into the coil and you may see a person crouched inside a metal cage, summoning all that electricity like a mad conductor.

⊙AMARU, ⊙NEW ZEALAND
STEAMPUNK HQ

YOU CAN'T MISS THIS

funky alternative future museum. A steam train with a dragon figurehead sits atop a pile of rubble out front, leading the way for the fantastical sights within. Steampunk is a genre of art and literature that combines imaginary Victorian-esque worlds with steam-powered technology. Cogs, gears, and machinery are assembled here into crazy contraptions that whir and clunk and do all sorts of things we can only dream about. Play the Metagalactic Pipe Organ or tinker with a light sculpture of glowing skulls. At Steampunk HQ, the possibilities are endless. Put on a pair of aviator biker goggles and let your imagination run wild.

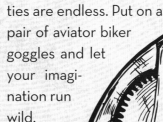

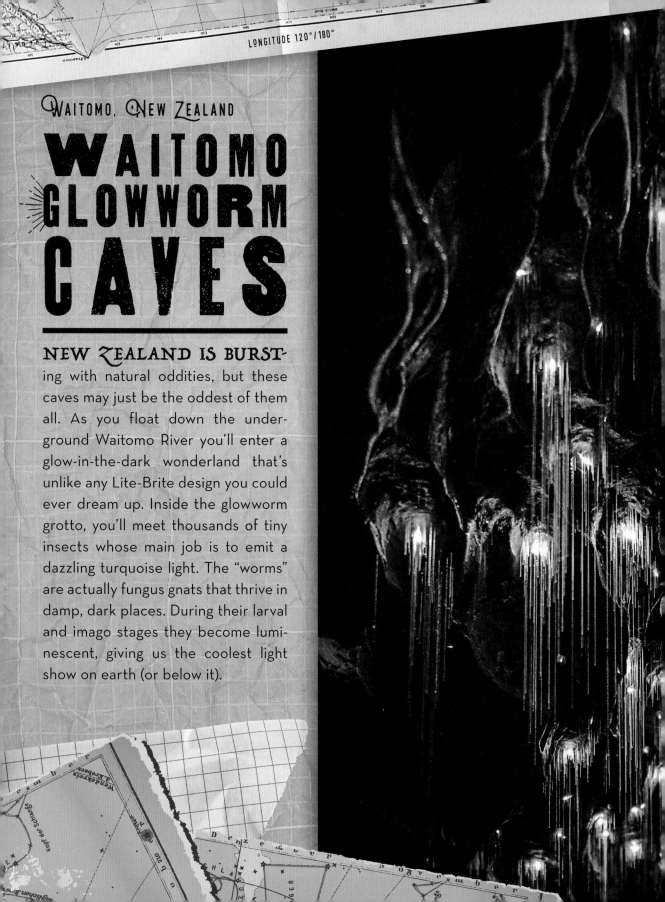

WAITOMO, NEW ZEALAND

WAITOMO GLOWWORM CAVES

NEW ZEALAND IS BURST-ing with natural oddities, but these caves may just be the oddest of them all. As you float down the underground Waitomo River you'll enter a glow-in-the-dark wonderland that's unlike any Lite-Brite design you could ever dream up. Inside the glowworm grotto, you'll meet thousands of tiny insects whose main job is to emit a dazzling turquoise light. The "worms" are actually fungus gnats that thrive in damp, dark places. During their larval and imago stages they become luminescent, giving us the coolest light show on earth (or below it).

WHANGANUI NATIONAL PARK, NEW ZEALAND

BRIDGE TO NOWHERE

THERE WERE HIGH HOPES for this bridge when it was built in 1936. Back then the remote Mangapurua Valley population was growing. Families were moving in, mostly soldiers returning from WWI, and farms were being hacked out of the thick vegetation on either side. But poor soil and the far reaches of the Great Depression drove people away. It didn't take long for the foliage to reclaim what once belonged to it. The bridge still stands but, true to its name, it won't actually lead you anywhere.

NEW ZEALAND

WHAKAARI (WHITE ISLAND)

Once described as "the worst hell on earth," White Island is the crater of an active volcano. There's absolutely no vegetation in this barren landscape, only patches of bright yellow sulphur crystals. The ground is covered in ash and cinder. The crater's lake is milky green and its water is more corrosive than battery acid! One wrong move here could send someone through the thin crust into pools of boiling mud or streams steeped with acid. The island grunts and hisses and spits, a constant reminder of the volcano that rules it.

Once upon a time, White Island was the site of a busy sulphur mine. But no man can tame this savage beast of a volcano: the mine stopped operating when part of the crater wall collapsed, killing 10 miners.

HAWKE'S BAY, NEW ZEALAND

TAUMATAWHAKA-TANGIHANGAKOAU-AUOTAMATEATURI-PUKAKAPIKIMAUN-GAHORONUKUPOKAI-WHENUAKITANATAHU

AT 85 LETTERS LONG, Taumata Hill (as it's known by locals) has been listed by the *Guinness Book of World Records* as the longest place name in the world. As the legend goes, the great Māori explorer Tamatea fought a battle on the hill. His beloved brother died in the clash, and Tamatea mourned his death by playing a *koauau* (a Māori flute) on the hill. The long name translates to "the summit where Tamatea, the man with the big knees, the slider, climber of mountains, the land-swallower who traveled about, played his nose flute to his loved one." Okay . . . now you try saying it!

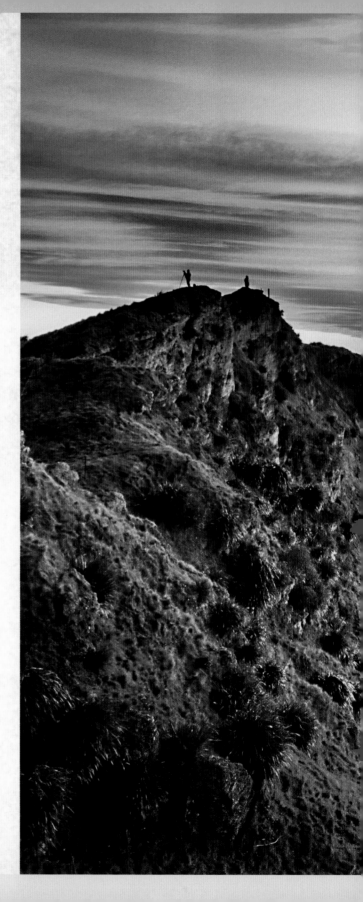

INDEX

PHOTO CREDITS

WanderDream/Shutterstock (bridge, and on p165) / p160-161: SM Rafiq Photography/Getty Images (Princess of Hope); evgenykz/Shutterstock (Bayterek) / p162-163: Novarc Images/Alamy (Karni Mata); Ru Bai Le/Shutterstock (prayer beads);SeanPavonePhoto/Getty Images (Kyaiktiyo Pagoda); GooseFrol/Shutterstock (elephant) / p164: humancode/Getty Images (photo) / p166-167: WanderDream/Shutterstock (photo) / p168: HelloRF Zcool/Shutterstock (photo) / p169: Brendan van Son/Shutterstock (photo left); Rat007/Shutterstock (photo right) / p170: Kiratsinh Jadeja/Getty Images (foreground photo); tanukiphoto/Getty Images (background photo) / p171: Aurora Photos/Alamy (photo) / p172: Phil Weymouth/Lonely Planet (seal); sivarock/Getty Images (dragon); Matt Munro/Lonely Planet (pig) / p173: Noppasin Wongchum/Alamy (photo); Christos Georghiou/Shutterstock (illustration) / p176-177: Daniela Dirscherl/Getty Images (large crab photo); Svetlana Turchenick/Shutterstock (small crab photo); thanit kanjananoppawong/Shutterstock (crab illustration); Mathieu Meur/Stocktrek Images/Getty Images (Grotto) / p178-179: Romas_Photo/Shutterstock (photo left); Golden Shrimp/Shutterstock (illustration); Chonlawut/Shutterstock (photo right) / p180-181: Alexandru Nika/Shutterstock (tree); Katvic/Shutterstock (coastline); Maks08/Shutterstock (Am Phu) / p182: Background Land/Shutterstock (wax drips); Zhukov Oleg/Shutterstock (house); ian woolcock/Shutterstock (photo) / p184-185: andrey oleynik/Shutterstock (illustration); Sony Herdiana/Shutterstock (photo) / p186: Stuart Forster/Alamy (photo); Andy Selinger/Alamy (stamps) / p187: Leonid Andronov/Shutterstock (Memorial Hall); Prachaya Roekdeethaweesab/Shutterstock (Mao) / p188-189: Jianhua Qiu/500px (cave) / p190-191: James Talalay/Alamy (photo); Kseniakrop/Shutterstock (illustration) / p192-193: Bodor Tivadar/Shutterstock (coffin, and on p196); IGOR MIHAJLOVIC/Shutterstock (geysers, and on p231); evenfh/Shutterstock (Rai Stones, and on p209); AVA Bitter/Shutterstock (cat, and on p214); Chansom Pantip/Shutterstock (vine, and on p199); Grassflowerhead/Shutterstock (island, and on p207); Emmanuel LATTES/Alamy (slug, and on p193); AkimD/Shutterstock (porthole, and on p206) / p194-195: matteo_it/Shutterstock (photo) / p196: raphme/Shutterstock (photo) / p197: Xinhua/Alamy (house); lynea/Shutterstock (chair) / p198: grebcha/Shutterstock (pitri dishes); DELstudio/Shutterstock (microscope) / p199: Tada Images/Shutterstock (Houtouwan) / p200: FotoGraphik/Getty Images (Rainbow Village); xpixel/Shutterstock (paint and brush) / p201: HD SIGNATURE CO.,LTD/Alamy (photo) / p202: leungchopan/Shutterstock (beach); gyro/iStockPhoto/Getty Images (sand); Trikona/Shutterstock (star) / p203: Sofiaworld/Shutterstock (photo); Danussa/Shutterstock (illustration) / p204-205: Torsten Pursche/Shutterstock (main photo); AustralianCamera/Shutterstock (smaller photo); Morphart Creation/Shutterstock (illustration) / p206: aminkorea/Shutterstock (submarine photo); Artur Balytskyi/Shutterstock (submarine illustration) / p207: flier-jodai/Getty Images (wooden interior) / p208: NH/Shutterstock (photo); eva_mask/Shutterstock (illustration) / p209: Stephen B. Goodwin/Shutterstock (stamps) / p210-211: Roland Nagy/Alamy (main photo) / p212: THPStock/Shutterstock (photo) / p213: imagevixen/Shutterstock (photo) / p214: Sankei/Getty Images (cats photo); Bodor Tivadar/Shutterstock (lower cat illustration) / p215: Nigel Killeen/Moment Editorial/Getty Images (cow sculpture); Rustic/Shutterstock (cow illustration) / p217: by Alla/Shutterstock (photo) / p218-219: Benny Marty/Shutterstock (photo); Utilisateur/Shutterstock (illustration) / p220: cachou44/iStockPhoto/Getty Images (photo); Morphart Creation/Shutterstock (illustration) / p221: paul abbitt rml/Alamy (photo); Separisa/Shutterstock (shark) / p222-223: imageBROKER/Alamy (photo) / p224: Martian977/Shutterstock (house); Umomos/Shutterstock (sign); Veniamin Kraskov/Shutterstock (protractor) / p225: Kai Schwoerer/Getty Images (photo); Olga Soloviova/Shutterstock (insect illustrations) / p226: pixelparticle/Shutterstock (Tesla coil) / p227: Bob Hilscher/Shutterstock (train); Naumov S/Shutterstock (bolts); Babich Alexander/Shutterstock (clockwork) / p228-229: Shaun Jeffers/Shutterstock (cave); Sergei Kardashev/Shutterstock (knots) / p230: Sebastian93 (photo) / p231: Kenishirotie/Shutterstock (batteries) / p232-233: Martian977/Shutterstock (photo); Sk_Advance studio/Shutterstock (illustration)

ACKNOWLEDGMENTS

Publishing Director: Piers Pickard / Publisher: Hanna Otero / Editor: Rhoda Belleza / Author: Nicole Maggi
Art Director: Ryan Thomann / Interior Designer: Gavin Motnyk / Print Production: Lisa Ford

Published in November 2019 by Lonely Planet Global Limited
CRN: 554153 / ISBN: 978-1-78868-326-5
www.lonelyplanetkids.com
© Lonely Planet 2019
2 4 6 8 10 9 7 5 3 1
Printed in Singapore

STAY IN TOUCH - lonelyplanet.com/contact
AUSTRALIA The Malt Store, Level 3, 551 Swanston St, Carlton, Victoria 3053
IRELAND Digital Depot, Roe Lane (off Thomas St), Digital Hub, Dublin 8, D08 TCV4, Ireland
UK 240 Blackfriars Rd, London SE1 8NW
USA 124 Linden St, Oakland, CA 94607